HOW TO MAKE
A MICHIGAN
WILL

Third Edition

—

Edward A. Haman
Mark Warda
Attorneys at Law

SPHINX® PUBLISHING
AN IMPRINT OF SOURCEBOOKS, INC.®
NAPERVILLE, ILLINOIS

Third Edition, 2002

Published by: **Sphinx® Publishing, An Imprint of Sourcebooks, Inc.®**

<u>Naperville Office</u>
P.O. Box 4410
Naperville, Illinois 60567-4410
630-961-3900
Fax: 630-961-2168
http://www.sourcebooks.com
http://www.sphinxlegal.com

This publication is designed to provide accurate and authoritative information in regard to the subject matter covered. It is sold with the understanding that the publisher is not engaged in rendering legal, accounting, or other professional service. If legal advice or other expert assistance is required, the services of a competent professional person should be sought.

From a Declaration of Principles Jointly Adopted by a Committee of the
American Bar Association and a Committee of Publishers and Associations

This product is not a substitute for legal advice.

Disclaimer required by Texas statutes.

Library of Congress Cataloging-in-Publication Data
Haman, Edward A.
    How to make a Michigan will / Edward A. Haman, Mark Warda.--3rd ed.
        p. cm.-- (Legal survival guides)
    Includes index.
    ISBN 1-57248-182-X
    1. Wills--Michigan--Popular works. 2. Inheritance and succession--Michigan--Popular works. I. Warda, Mark. II. Title. III. Series.

KFM4344.Z9 H36 2002
346.77405'4--dc21
                                                          2001049009

Printed and bound in the United States of America.

VHG Paperback — 10 9 8 7 6 5 4 3 2 1

CONTENTS

Using Self-Help Law Books

Before using a self-help law book, you should realize the advantages and disadvantages of doing your own legal work and understand the challenges and diligence that this requires.

THE GROWING TREND

Rest assured that you won't be the first or only person handling your own legal matter. For example, in some states, more than seventy-five percent of divorces and other cases have at least one party representing him or herself. Because of the high cost of legal services, this is a major trend and many courts are struggling to make it easier for people to represent themselves. However, some courts are not happy with people who do not use attorneys and refuse to help them in any way. For some, the attitude is, "Go to the law library and figure it out for yourself."

We at Sphinx write and publish self-help law books to give people an alternative to the often complicated and confusing legal books found in most law libraries. We have made the explanations of the law as simple and easy to understand as possible. Of course, unlike an attorney advising an individual client, we cannot cover every conceivable possibility.

COST/VALUE ANALYSIS

Whenever you shop for a product or service, you are faced with various levels of quality and price. In deciding what product or service to buy, you make a cost/value analysis on the basis of your willingness to pay and the quality you desire.

When buying a car, you decide whether you want transportation, comfort, status, or sex appeal. Accordingly, you decide among such choices as a Neon, a Lincoln, a Rolls Royce, or a Porsche. Before making a decision, you usually weigh the merits of each option against the cost.

When you get a headache, you can take a pain reliever (such as aspirin) or visit a medical specialist for a neurological examination. Given this choice, most people, of course, take a pain reliever, since it costs only pennies; whereas a medical examination costs hundreds of dollars and takes a lot of time. This is usually a logical choice because it is rare to need anything more than a pain reliever for a headache. But in some cases, a headache may indicate a brain tumor and failing to see a specialist right away can result in complications. Should everyone with a headache go to a specialist? Of course not, but people treating their own illnesses must realize that they are betting on the basis of their cost/value analysis of the situation. They are taking the most logical option.

The same cost/value analysis must be made when deciding to do one's own legal work. Many legal situations are very straight forward, requiring a simple form and no complicated analysis. Anyone with a little intelligence and a book of instructions can handle the matter without outside help.

But there is always the chance that complications are involved that only an attorney would notice. To simplify the law into a book like this, several legal cases often must be condensed into a single sentence or paragraph. Otherwise, the book would be several hundred pages long and too complicated for most people. However, this simplification necessarily leaves out many details and nuances that would apply to special or unusual situations. Also, there are many ways to interpret most legal questions. Your case may come before a judge who disagrees with the analysis of our authors.

Therefore, in deciding to use a self-help law book and to do your own legal work, you must realize that you are making a cost/value analysis. You have decided that the money you will save in doing it yourself outweighs the chance that your case will not turn out to your satisfaction. Most people handling their own simple legal matters never have a problem, but occasionally people find that it ended up costing them more to have an attorney straighten out the situation than it would have if they had hired an attorney in the beginning. Keep this in mind if you decide to handle your own case, and be sure to consult an attorney if you feel you might need further guidance.

LOCAL RULES   The next thing to remember is that a book which covers the law for the entire nation, or even for an entire state, cannot possibly include every procedural difference of every county court. Whenever possible, we provide the exact form needed; however, in some areas, each county, or even each judge, may require unique forms and procedures. In our *state* books, our forms usually cover the majority of counties in the state, or provide examples of the type of form that will be required. In our *national* books, our forms are sometimes even more general in nature but are designed to give a good idea of the type of form that will be needed in most locations. Nonetheless, keep in mind that your *state*, county, or judge may have a requirement, or use a form, that is not included in this book.

You should not necessarily expect to be able to get all of the information and resources you need solely from within the pages of this book. This book will serve as your guide, giving you specific information whenever possible and helping you to find out what else you will need to know. This is just like if you decided to build your own backyard deck. You might purchase a book on how to build decks. However, such a book would not include the building codes and permit requirements of every city, town, county, and township in the nation; nor would it include the lumber, nails, saws, hammers, and other materials and tools you would need to actually build the deck. You would use the book as your guide, and then do some work and research involving such matters as whether you need a permit of some kind, what type and grade of wood are available in your area, whether to use hand tools or power tools, and how to use those tools.

Before using the forms in a book like this, you should check with your court clerk to see if there are any local rules of which you should be aware, or local forms you will need to use. Often, such forms will require the same information as the forms in the book but are merely laid out differently, use slightly different language, or use different color paper so the clerks can easily find them. They will sometimes require additional information.

CHANGES IN THE LAW

Besides being subject to state and local rules and practices, the law is subject to change at any time. The courts and the legislatures of all fifty states are constantly revising the laws. It is possible that while you are reading this book, some aspect of the law is being changed or that a court is interpreting a law in a different way. You should always check the most recent statutes, rules and regulations to see what, if any changes have been made.

In most cases, the change will be of minimal significance. A form will be redesigned, additional information will be required, or a waiting period will be extended. As a result, you might need to revise a form, file an extra form, or wait out a longer time period; these types of changes will not usually affect the outcome of your case. On the other hand, sometimes a major part of the law is changed, the entire law in a particular area is rewritten, or a case that was the basis of a central legal point is overruled. In such instances, your entire ability to pursue your case may be impaired.

To help you with local requirements and changes in the law, be sure to read the section in Chapter 1 on "Legal Research."

Again, you should weigh the value of your case against the cost of an attorney and make a decision as to what you believe is in your best interest.

INTRODUCTION

This book is intended to give Michigan residents a basic understanding of the laws regarding wills, joint property, and other types of ownership of property as they affect their estate planning. It is designed to allow those with simple estates to quickly and inexpensively set up their affairs to distribute their property according to their wishes.

It also includes information on appointing a guardian and conservator for minor children. This can be useful in avoiding bad feelings between relatives and in protecting the children from being raised by someone you would object to raising them.

Chapters 1 through 7 explain the Michigan laws regarding wills, the passing of property at death, living wills, and making anatomical gifts. There is a glossary after Chapter 7 to help you with some legal terms. Appendix A contains selected sections of the Michigan laws relating to wills, probate, and living wills. These sections are explained in this book, however, sometimes it is helpful to read the law exactly as it is written.

Appendix B contains sample filled-in forms to give you an idea of what some of the forms look like when completed. Appendix C contains blank forms you can use. A chart in Appendix C will help you choose the right form based upon your circumstances and desires.

You can prepare your own will quickly and easily by using the forms out of this book by photocopying them, or you can retype the material on blank paper. The small amount of time it takes to do this can give you and your loved ones the peace of mind of knowing that your estate will be distributed according to your wishes.

A surprising number of people have had their estates pass to the wrong parties because of a simple lack of knowledge of how the laws work. Before using any of the forms in Appendix B, you should read and understand the information in Chapters 1 through 7 of this book.

Making a will involves thinking about who you would like to give your property to in the event you die now. It also involves thinking about how things could change after you have made your will. It is a matter of making contingency plans. For example, if you are married and have minor children, you should ask questions like: "What if my spouse died first?" or "What if my children were grown up?" The answer to the question of how you want your property divided might be different in such situations.

If your situation is at all complicated, you should seek the advice of an attorney. In many communities, wills can be prepared by an attorney for a very reasonable price. No book of this type can cover every contingency in every case, but a knowledge of the basics will help you to make the right decisions regarding your property.

The forms in this book are for simple wills to leave property to your family, friends, or charities. If you wish to disinherit your family and leave your property to others, you should consult with an attorney who can be sure that your will cannot be successfully challenged in court.

KNOWING THE BASIC RULES

1

Before making your will, you should understand how a will works and what it can and cannot accomplish. Otherwise, your plans may not be carried out and the wrong people may end up with your property.

WILL DEFINED

A *will* is a document in which you state who should get your property when you die, and who will manage your estate upon your death. If you have minor children, it can also be used to determine who will have custody of them and their property. If you do not express your wishes in a will, the laws of the State of Michigan will decide these matters.

HOW A WILL IS USED

Some people think that a will avoids *probate*; it does not. Probate is the process of settling an estate after someone's death. A will is the document used in probate to determine who receives the property, who is appointed to manage your estate, and who is appointed guardian and conservator of minor children.

THE PROBATE PROCESS

The details of how to probate an estate is beyond the scope of this book, however, we will give a brief explanation of what is involved in the probate process. Most people are under the misconception that probate is a horribly complex and lengthy process that is best avoided at all cost. In reality, for many people, probate is preferable to complexity or potential risk of the various techniques for avoiding probate.

When a person dies, his or her will is filed with the Probate Court in the county where the person resided. Various court papers are prepared and filed, such as: a *petition for probate* (this is a formal request for the court to recognize the will, appoint a personal representative, and oversee the probate of the estate), and a list of the person's assets.

Once appointed by the court, the *personal representative* is then responsible for paying any debts of the decedent, and distributing the remaining assets to the beneficiaries as directed by the will. The personal representative pays known debts, and places an ad in a local newspaper which is considered notice for anyone else to submit claims against the estate within a certain number of days. As for paying the debts, the personal representative uses only the assets of the decedent. Neither the personal representative, nor any family member or beneficiary of the decedent, are personally responsible for any of the decedent's debts (unless, of course, they are joint debtors with the decedent).

The personal representative then files a report indicating what was taken in and paid out of the estate, and obtains an order closing the estate. Much of the work is actually done by an attorney hired by the personal representative, although it is possible to do this without a lawyer.

Standardized probate forms may be found in a two-volume set of books, published by the Michigan State Court Administrators Office, called Michigan S.C.A.O. Approved Forms, which will be available at your nearest law library.

AVOIDING
PROBATE

If you wish to avoid probate, you need to use methods other than a will, such as joint ownership, pay-on-death accounts, or living trusts. Avoiding probate through joint ownership of property and pay-on-death accounts is discussed later in this chapter. For information on living trusts, you should refer to a book that focuses on trusts used for estate planning.

It can be argued that you may not need a will if you can successfully avoid probate for all of your property (and do not need to designate a guardian or conservator for any minor children). In many cases, when a husband or wife dies and everything is jointly owned, no will or probate is necessary. However, everyone should have a will in case some property is subject to probate. This might happen if you and your spouse forgot to put some property into joint ownership, if you received property just before death, or if you and your spouse die at the same time.

IF YOU DO NOT HAVE A WILL

If you do not have a will, Michigan law will determine how your property will be divided.(Michigan Compiled Laws Annotated (Mich. Comp. Laws Ann.), Sections (Secs.) 700.2102 through 700.2109 and Michigan Statutes Annotated (Mich. Stat. Ann.), Secs. 27.12102 through 27.12109.) According to this law (also called the *law of intestate succession*), your property would be distributed as follows:

1. If you leave a spouse, and have no living children or parents, your spouse gets your entire estate.

2. If you leave a spouse, have no children, but at least one of your parents survives, your spouse gets the first $150,000 plus three-fourths of the balance of your estate. The other one-fourth of the balance goes to your parent or parents.

3. If you leave a spouse and children who are all children of you and your spouse, and your spouse has no other surviving children (such as from a prior marriage), your spouse gets the first $150,000 plus one-half of the balance. The children get equal shares of the other one-half.

4. If you leave a spouse and children who are all children of you and your spouse, and your spouse has at least one child who is not yours, your spouse gets the first $150,000 plus one-half of the balance. Your children get the other one-half of the balance.

5. If you leave a spouse and children who are all children of you and your spouse, and you also have any children who are not your spouse's child (such as from your prior marriage), your spouse gets the first

$150,000 plus one-half of the balance. Your children get the other one-half of the balance.

6. If you leave a spouse with whom you do not have any children, and you have children (such as from a prior marriage), your spouse gets the first $100,000 plus one-half of the balance. Your children get the other one-half of the balance.

7. If you do not leave a spouse, but have children, your children get equal shares of your estate.

8. If you leave no spouse and no children, then your estate would go to the highest ranking living person or persons on the following list (these are listed in order, beginning with the highest rank):

    a. your parents;

    b. any descendents of your parents;

    c. your grandparents, with one-half going to your maternal grandparents and one-half to your paternal grandparents. If both grandparents on one side are deceased, their share goes to their descendents. If there are no surviving grandparents or their descendents on one side, the entire estate goes to the surviving grandparents or their descendents on the other side; or,

    d. the State of Michigan.

If you leave a wife, she will need to choose between the provisions listed above and her rights under another provision of Michigan law. (Mich. Comp. Laws Ann., Secs. 558.1 through 558.29 and Mich. Stat. Ann., Secs. 26.221 through 26.245.) This other provision relates to a widow's *dower rights*. Dower rights only apply to a surviving wife; not to a surviving husband. Dower rights are discussed further on page 6 of this book, and statutes relating to dower rights may be found in Appendix A.

JOINT TENANCY, SPOUSES, AND WILLS

Holding property jointly with others, or being married, can affect what you can and cannot do in a will. This section will explain this.

JOINT TENANCY
OVERRULES A
WILL

As used in this book, the terms *joint tenancy* and *joint ownership* refer to *joint tenancy with full rights of survivorship*. On a bank account this would be designated by the word "or" between the names of the two owners. On a deed to real estate, and often on other types of property, the names of the joint owners would be followed by the phrase "as joint tenants with full rights of survivorship." If the property were to be titled as *tenants in common* (using the word "and" on a bank account), then one-half of the property would go to the joint owner and one-half of the property would pass under the will.

When a will gives property to one person, but that property is already jointly owned with another person, the will is ignored and the joint owner gets the property. This is because the jointly owned property avoids probate and passes directly to the joint owner. A will only controls property which goes through probate.

Example 1: Bill's will leaves all of his property to his wife, Mary. Bill dies owning a house jointly with his sister, Joan, and a bank account jointly with his son, Don. Joan gets the house; Don gets the bank account; and his wife, Mary, gets nothing.

Example 2: Betty's will leaves one-half of her assets to Ann and one-half of her assets to George. Betty dies owning $1,000,000 in stock jointly with George, and a car in her own name. Ann gets only a one-half interest in the car. George gets all of the stock and one-half of the car.

Example 3: John's will leaves all of his property equally to his five children. Before going in the hospital he makes his oldest son, Harry, the joint owner of his accounts. John dies and Harry gets all of his assets. The rest of the children get nothing.

In each of these cases the property went to a person it should not have, because the decedent did not realize that joint ownership overruled the will. In some families this might not be a problem. Harry might divide up the property equally (and possibly pay a gift tax). But in many cases Harry would just keep everything and the family would never talk to him again, or would take him to court.

A SPOUSE CAN
OVERRULE A
WILL

Under Michigan law, a surviving spouse is entitled to a certain portion of the decedent's estate no matter what the will says. (Mich. Comp. Laws Ann., Secs. 700.2201 and 700.2202, and Mich. Stat. Ann., Sec. 27.12201 and 27.12202.) This is sometimes called the *elective share*, or the *forced share*. The elective share can be claimed even if the will specifically says the spouse is to receive nothing. The spouse is not required to take this share, but may elect to do so.

The elective share in Michigan is one-half of what the spouse would have received if there had not been a will, reduced by one-half of what the spouse received outside of probate (such as joint property and life insurance). If the surviving spouse is a woman, she could instead take dower rights, which is the use (i.e., a *life estate*) of one-third of all land owned by her deceased husband. (Mich. Comp. Laws Ann., Secs. 558.1 through 558.29 and Mich. Stat. Ann., Secs. 26.221 through 26.245.)

The following examples assume the surviving spouse makes this election to take one-half of what he or she would have received if there had not been a will.

Example 1: John's will leaves all of his property to his children of a prior marriage and nothing to his wife who is already wealthy. The wife still gets 25% of John's estate and his children divide up the remaining 75%.

Example 2: Mary (who has no children) puts one-half of her property in a joint account with her husband, and in her will she leaves all of her other property to her sister. When she dies her husband gets all of the money in the joint account *and* one-half of her other property. Mary's sister only gets half of what Mary intended her to receive.

JOINT TENANCY OVERRULES A SPOUSE'S ELECTIVE SHARE

One way to avoid a spouse's elective share is to have all property in joint ownership with others. Other ways are to set up a trust, or to sign an agreement with your spouse either before or after the marriage.

Example: Dan owns his stocks jointly with his son. He owns his bank accounts jointly with his daughter. If he has no other property, his spouse gets nothing since there is no property in his probate estate.

JOINT TENANCY IS RISKY

The above cases may make it appear that joint tenancy is the answer to all problems, but it often creates even more problems. If you put your real estate in joint ownership with someone, you cannot sell it or mortgage it without that person's signature. If you put your bank account in joint ownership with someone, they can take all of your money out.

Example 1: Alice put her house in joint ownership with her son. She later married Ed and moved in with him. She wanted to sell her house and to invest the proceeds from the sale for income. Her son refused to sign the deed. She was in court for ten months clearing the title and the judge almost refused to do it.

Example 2: Alex put his bank accounts into joint ownership with his daughter, Mary. Mary fell in love with Doug who was in trouble with the law. Doug talked Mary into "borrowing" $30,000 from the account for a "business deal" that later went sour. Later she "borrowed" $25,000 more to pay Doug's bail bond. Alex did not find out until it was too late and his money was gone.

BANK ACCOUNTS AND SECURITIES

There are various ways in which bank accounts and securities accounts can avoid probate and a spouse's elective share. You should consult an attorney if you have many of these accounts and this section does not cover your situation.

I/T/F BANK ACCOUNTS

One way to keep bank accounts out of your probate estate, avoid a spouse's elective share, and still retain control is to title them *in trust for* or *I/T/F*, with a named beneficiary. No one but you can get the money until your death, and on death it immediately and automatically goes directly to the person you name, without a will or probate proceeding. This is sometimes called a *Totten Trust*, named after the court case that declared them legal.

You may also be able to open a bank account in your name alone, and designate a beneficiary to get the account automatically upon your death. This is commonly called a *pay on death* or *transfer on death* account. This has the same effect as a traditional Totten Trust account. Your bank can advise you on what is available.

Example: Rich opened a bank account in the name of "Rich, I/T/F Mary." If Rich dies, the money automatically goes to Mary, but prior to Rich's death Mary has no control over the account, does not even have to know about it, and Rich can take Mary's name off the account at any time.

PAY-ON-DEATH BANK AND SECURITY ACCOUNTS

Until recently, the Totten Trust concept only applied to bank accounts. Stocks, bonds, and other securities still had to go though probate. Michigan has now joined twenty-six other states in enacting laws permitting *pay on death* (or *POD*) or *transfer on death* (or *TOD*) accounts for securities. (Mich. Comp. Laws Ann., Secs. 700.6302 through 700.6310 and Mich. Stat. Ann., Sec. 27.16302 through 27.16310.) These include stocks, bonds, mutual funds, and other similar investments.

To set up your securities to transfer automatically upon death, you need to have them correctly registered. If you use a brokerage account, the brokerage company should have a form for you to do this.

If your securities are currently registered in your own name, or with your spouse, you would need to re-register them in the transfer on death format with the designation of your beneficiary.

The following are examples of how accounts may be designated ("JT TEN" means *joint tenants*):

Sole owner with sole beneficiary:

    John S. Brown TOD John S. Brown, Jr.

Multiple owners with sole beneficiary (John and Mary are joint tenants with right of survivorship and when they die, John, Jr., inherits the securities):

    John S. Brown and Mary B. Brown JT TEN TOD
    John S. Brown, Jr.

Multiple owners with beneficiary and substituted beneficiary (John and Mary are joint tenants with right of survivorship, and when they die John, Jr., inherits the securities, but if John, Jr. dies first then Peter inherits):

    John S. Brown and Mary B. Brown JT TEN TOD
    John S. Brown, Jr., SUB BENE Peter Q. Brown.

Multiple owners; to beneficiary or lineal descendants (John and Mary are joint tenants and when they die, John, Jr. inherits, but if John Jr., dies first, then John Jr.'s lineal descendants inherit. "LPDS" means *lineal descendants per stirpes*):

    John S. Brown and Mary B. Brown JT TEN TOD
    John S. Brown, Jr. LDPS.

EXEMPTIONS

Michigan law provides for certain property to be *exempt* from being controlled by a will. If you have a spouse, your spouse gets this property; and if you have no spouse, your children get it. To avoid having property declared exempt, it may be specifically given to someone in a will. If certain items are specifically given to certain persons, those items will not be considered part of the exempt property. If cash is kept in a joint or I/T/F bank account, it would go to the joint owner or beneficiary and not be used as the family allowance.

The three main exemptions are:

1. homestead allowance under Michigan Compiled Laws Annotated, Section 700.2402 and Michigan Statutes Annotated, Section 27.1402;

2. exempt property under Michigan Compiled Laws Annotated, Section 700.2404 and Michigan Statutes Annotated, Section 27.12404; and,

3. family allowance under Michigan Compiled Laws Annotated, Section 700.2403 and Michigan Statutes Annotated, Section 27.12403.

Each of these are briefly explained below. These are simplified explanations. If you need to find out more details about these exemptions, start by reading the provisions in the Michigan law designated after each of the categories above.

HOMESTEAD
ALLOWANCE

A surviving spouse is entitled to receive $10,000 as a *homestead allowance*. If there is no surviving spouse, each minor child of the decedent is entitled to a homestead allowance equal to $10,000 divided by the number of minor children. However, if the homestead allowance would be less than what the surviving spouse or minor children would receive under the will or by law, it will be charged against the amount received under the will or by law. The homestead allowance is provided for in Michigan Compiled Laws Annotated, Section 700.2402 and Michigan Statutes Annotated, Section 27.12402.

Example 1: George dies with a will giving his wife $75,000. Since the homestead allowance of $10,000 would be less than the $75,000 under the will, George's wife will not get the homestead allowance.

Example 2: George dies with a will giving his wife $5,000. Since the homestead allowance of $10,000 would be more than the $5,000 under the will, George's wife gets $15,000 (the $5,000 under the will plus the $10,000 homestead allowance).

EXEMPT
PROPERTY

In addition to the homestead allowance, a surviving spouse is also entitled to receive, as *exempt property*, up to $3,500 in excess of any security interest (money owed on the property), in household furniture, furnishings, appliances, and personal effects. If there is no surviving spouse, the minor children of the decedent are entitled to the exempt property (to a total of $3,500; not $3,500 for each child). Exempt property is provided for in Michigan Compiled Laws Annotated, Section 700.2404 and Michigan Statutes Annotated, Section 27.12404.

FAMILY
ALLOWANCE

A *family allowance* may also be permitted when there is a surviving spouse or minor children whom the decedent was legally obligated to support. Whether a family allowance is permitted, and the amount and duration of the allowance, is determined by the court on a case-by-case basis. The family allowance is provided for in Michigan Compiled Laws Annotated, Section 700.2403 and Michigan Statutes Annotated, Section 27.12403.

MARRIAGE AND YOUR WILL

If you get married after making your will and do not make a new will or codicil after the wedding, your spouse gets a share of your estate as if you had no will, unless you:

- have a pre-nuptial agreement;

- made a provision for your spouse in the will; or,

- stated in your will that you intended not to mention your prospective spouse. (Mich. Comp. Laws Ann., Sec. 700.2301 and Mich. Stat. Ann., Sec. 27.12301.)

Example: John made out his will leaving everything to his disabled brother. John later married Joan, an heiress with plenty of money, but did not change his will as he still wanted his brother to get his estate. When he died Joan got his entire estate and his brother got nothing.

CHILDREN AND YOUR WILL

If you have a child after making your will and do not make a new will or codicil, the child gets a share of your estate as if there was no will. (Mich. Comp. Laws Ann., Sec. 700.2302 and Mich. Stat. Ann., Sec. 27.12302.)

Example: Dave made a will leaving one-half of his estate to his sister and the other one-half to be shared by his three children. He later has another child but does not revise his will. Upon his death, his fourth child would get one quarter of his estate, his sister would get three-eighths, and the other three children would each get one-eighth.

It is best to rewrite your will at the birth of a child. However, another solution is to include the following clause after the names of your children in your will:

```
"...and any afterborn children living at the time
of my death, in equal shares."
```

If you have one or more children and are leaving all of your property to your spouse, then your will would not be affected by the subsequent birth of a child.

YOUR DEBTS

One of the duties of the person administering an estate is to pay the debts of the decedent. Before an estate is distributed, the legitimate debts must be ascertained and paid.

An exception is made for *secured* debts. These are debts that are protected by a lien against property, such as a home mortgage or car loan. In the case of a secured debt, the loan does not have to be paid before the property is distributed. This is because the debt follows the property to the new owner.

Example: John owns a $100,000 house with an $80,000 mortgage, and has $100,000 in the bank. If he leaves the house to his brother and the bank account to his sister, then his brother would receive the house but would owe the $80,000 mortgage.

What if your debts are more than the value of your property? Today, unlike years ago, people cannot inherit the debt of another. A person's property is used to pay their probate and funeral expenses first, and if there is not enough left to pay their other debts, then the creditors are out of luck. However, if a person leaves property to someone and does not have enough assets to pay his or her debts, then the property will be sold to pay the debts.

Example: Jeb's will leaves all of his property to his three children. At the time of his death, Jeb has $30,000 in medical bills, $11,000 in credit card debt. His only assets are his $2,000 car and $5,000 in stock. The car and stock would be sold and the funeral bill and probate fees paid out of the proceeds. If any money was left, it would go to the creditors and nothing would be left for the children. However, the children would *not* have to pay the balance owed to the creditors.

ESTATE AND INHERITANCE TAXES

FEDERAL ESTATE
AND GIFT TAX

Under the Federal Estate and Gift Tax, there is a tax on estates with assets valued above a certain amount. Estates below that amount are allowed a *unified credit* which exempts them from tax. The unified credit applies to the combination of the estate a person leaves at death and gifts made during the person's lifetime.

When a person makes a gift, the amount of the gift is subtracted from the total unified credit to which he or she is entitled. Any amount remaining after all lifetime gifts are subtracted is the amount that will be exempt from tax upon death. However, a person is allowed to make gifts of up to $11,000 per person, per year without having them subtracted from the unified credit. This means that a married couple can make gifts of up to $22,000 per year with no tax effect. The Taxpayer Relief Act of 1997 provided that this exclusion amount will be adjusted for inflation.

In 1998, the amount exempted by the unified credit was $625,000, but it will rise to $1,000,000 by the year 2006 (barring any changes by Congress). Under current law, the amount will change according to the following schedule:

Year	Amount
2002-2003	$ 700,000
2004	$ 850,000
2005	$ 950,000
2006	$1,000,000

MICHIGAN
TAXES

Michigan has an inheritance tax. It is a somewhat complex tax. (Mich. Stat. Ann., Sec. 7.561 and Mich. Comp. Laws Ann., Sec. 205.201.) It taxes estates based on a graduated percentage of the estate's value. The tax rate begins at 2% of estates valued at $100 to $50,000; and tops out at 10% on estates over $750,000. However, there are numerous exemptions, including a $50,000 exemption for transfers to certain family members, and $65,000 for transfers to a spouse. This is only a very basic summary of the tax. See the provisions in the law, or consult an attorney if you are concerned about estate tax planning.

LEGAL RESEARCH

This book is designed to give a vast majority of people all the information required to make their own will. If you have a sizeable estate, want to do tax planning with your will, desire to set up complicated trusts, or wish to deal with any other complicated matters, you should consult an experienced lawyer. If you want to do some more research on your own, you will need to visit your nearest law library. One may usually be found in or near the courthouse for your county. Ask the court clerk's office for the location of the law library. Law libraries may also be found at law schools. These libraries may have restrictions on use by the general public, so it is a good idea to call first.

The basic laws for Michigan are the laws passed by the Michigan Legislature. These are compiled in a set of books called Michigan Compiled Laws Annotated (abbreviated in this book as Mich. Comp. Laws Ann.).

NOTE: *The official way that lawyers and judges abbreviate the Michigan Compiled Laws Annotated is M.C.L.A. However, this book will abbreviate as stated above so you will remember what the law is called.*

Laws on wills and probate are primarily found beginning at Section 700.1101. In addition to a library or law library, you may also access the Michigan Compiled Laws Annotated online at:

http://MichiganLegislature.org/law/Default.asp.

This site also contains other information about the Michigan Legislature, including pending bills and recent changes in the law that have not yet been appeared in the Michigan Compiled Laws Annotated. One other source of online legal information is:

http://www.findlaw.com

This site has links to legal information for all fifty states and the District of Columbia.

Another good source of information is a book entitled *Planning for Estates and Administration in Michigan*, by Frederick K. Hoops; which is Volume 1 of the four-volume *Michigan Practice Library* series published by Lawyers Cooperative Publishing. Look for sections 6:1 to 6:344. Also, section 45:24 in Volume 4 discusses anatomical gifts.

Other books you may find helpful include:

- *Michigan Estate Planning, Will Drafting and Estate Administration*, by Joyce Q. Lower and Henry M. Grix; Aspen Publications.

- *Michigan Will Drafting*, by Michael E. Irish and John H. Martin; Michigan Institute for Continuing Legal Education.

You may also find a set of books called Michigan Statutes Annotated (abbreviated in this book as Mich. Stat. Ann.), which uses a different numbering system. The will and probate laws begin at Section 27.11101. The Michigan Statutes Annotated is being phased out, and no new laws passed by the Michigan Legislature are being assigned Michigan Statutes Annotated. numbers.

NOTE: *The official way that lawyers and judges abbreviate the Michigan Statutes is M.S.A. However, this book will abbreviate as stated above so you will remember what the law is called.*

Both sets of books have volumes containing tables that cross-reference the Michigan Compiled Laws Annotated and Michigan Statutes Annotated section numbers. References to the section numbers of both sets are used in this book whenever possible.

DECIDING IF YOU NEED A MICHIGAN WILL 2

Any person who is at least eighteen years of age and of sound mind can make a will in Michigan. However, this chapter will help you understand what a will does or does not do, and who is involved in or affected by wills. Then you can decide if you need one.

WHAT A WILL CAN DO

There are several things that can be accomplished with a will, and there are many people involved.

BENEFICIARIES

A will allows you to decide who gets your property after your death. Those to whom you leave property are called *beneficiaries*. You can give specific personal items to certain persons and choose which of your friends or relatives, if any, deserve a greater share of your estate. You can leave gifts to schools, charities, and other organizations.

PERSONAL REPRESENTATIVE

A will also allows you to decide who will be in charge of handling your estate. This is the person who gathers together all of your assets and distributes them to creditors and beneficiaries, hires attorneys and accountants if necessary, and files any essential tax or probate forms. This person is called a *personal representative*. Such a person may also be called an *administrator* or *administratrix* (if there is not a will), or an *executor* or *executrix* (if appointed by a will).

With a will you can provide that your personal representative does not have to post a surety bond with the court in order to serve, which can save your estate some money. You can also give your personal representative the power to sell your property and take other actions without first getting a court order.

GUARDIAN AND
CONSERVATOR

A will also allows you to choose a *guardian* and *conservator* for your minor children. A guardian makes the types of decisions a parent would regarding the child; and a conservator handles the child's money and assets. This way you can avoid fights among relatives and make sure the best person raises your children. You may also appoint separate persons as guardian over your children and conservator over their money. For example you may appoint your sister as guardian over your children and your father as conservator over their money. That way a second person could keep an eye on how their money was being spent. Also, one person may be better at parenting, and another better at managing money.

TRUSTS

You can also set up a trust to provide that your property is not distributed immediately. Many people feel that their children would not be ready to handle large sums of money at the age of eighteen, or even older. A will can direct that the money be held and managed by a trustee until the children are older.

MINIMIZING
TAXES

A trust created in a will is called a *testamentary trust*. Form 6 and form 13 in Appendix C of this book contain simple testamentary trust provisions. You may also create a trust that is separate from your will, which will probably be more complex than the basic trust provisions contained in the forms in this book.

A trust created separate from a will is called a *living trust* or an *inter vivos trust*. How to create a separate, or a more complex, trust is beyond the scope of this book. However, we will discuss some basic information about trusts so that you can decide whether you want to pursue this option.

A trust is created by a document that sets forth the terms of the trust. This can be done by either creating a trust document that is separate from your will, or by creating a trust in your will. The provisions of a trust document will include designating a trustee and the beneficiaries. It may also set forth such matters as:

- how and when the income and assets of the trust are to be distributed to the beneficiaries;

- guidelines for how the trustee is to invest the trust assets to generate income;

- what happens if the trustee can no longer serve; and

- what happens if any of the beneficiaries die.

If you create a trust document that is separate from your will, some assets will need to be transferred to the trust. For tax purposes, the trust will be separate from your personal taxes, and will have to file a separate tax return. If you already have a trust, you can provide in your will that some or all of your estate go into the trust upon your death (Mich, Comp. Laws Ann., Sec. 700.2511; Mich, Stat. Ann, Sec. 27.12511.)

If your estate is over the amount protected by the federal unified credit (see the section in Chapter 1 on "Estate and Inheritance Taxes"), then it will be subject to the Federal Estate and Gift Tax. If you wish to lower the taxes, for example, by making gifts to charities, you can do so through a will. However, such estate planning is beyond the scope of this book and you should consult an estate planning attorney or another book for further information.

WHAT A WILL CANNOT DO

A will cannot direct that anything illegal be done, and it cannot put unreasonable conditions on a gift. For example, a provision that your daughter gets all of your property only if she divorces her husband would be ignored by the court. She would get the property with no conditions attached. You can put some conditions in your will, but to be certain they can be enforced you should consult an attorney.

A will cannot leave money or property to an animal because animals cannot legally own property. If you wish to continue paying for the care of a pet after your death, you should leave the animal to someone you trust will care for it, and leave funds to that person *in trust* for the pet's care.

OUT-OF-STATE WILLS

A will that is valid in another state would probably be valid to pass property in Michigan. However, before such a will could be accepted by a Michigan Probate Court, one of the witnesses to your will, or another person in your former state, would have to testify to the validity of the signature on your will. Because of the expense and delay in finding out-of-state witnesses, it is advisable to execute a new will after moving to Michigan.

Another advantage to having a Michigan will is that, as a Michigan resident, your estate will only be concerned with Michigan state probate or inheritance taxes. If you move to Michigan but keep your old will, your former state of residence may try to collect taxes on your estate.

If you reside in Michigan part of the year and in another state the other part of the year, and you own substantial property in each state, a question can arise as to the best state in which to execute your will. Most people would execute their will in the state they regard as their primary state of residence (the state where they have their drivers license, are registered to vote, would like to be buried, etc.). Upon death it would be necessary for the Michigan property to be probated in the Michigan courts, and the property in the other state would have to be probated in the courts of that state (unless probate avoidance techniques are employed such as the use of joint property or trusts).

One complication may arise if the other state has a much lower inheritance tax, or even no inheritance tax. In such a case, depending upon how much of your property is in the other state, it may be advisable to switch your primary state of residence, and even to rearrange your assets. If you think you may be in this situation, you should consult an attorney.

WHO CAN USE A SIMPLE WILL

The wills in this book will pass your property whether your estate is $1,000 or $100,000,000. However, if your estate is over the amount of the unified credit (see the section on "Estate and Inheritance Taxes" in Chapter 1), then you might be able to avoid estate taxes by using a trust or other tax-saving device. The larger your estate, the more you can save on estate taxes by doing more complicated estate planning. If you have a large estate and are concerned about estate taxes, you should consult an estate planning attorney or a book on estate planning.

WHO SHOULD NOT USE A SIMPLE WILL

A simple will should not be used by everyone. The following will explain some situations in which you may run into problems if you use a simple will.

WILL CONTEST

If you expect that there may be a fight over your estate, or that someone might contest the validity of your will, then your should consult a lawyer. If you leave less than the statutory elective share of your estate to your spouse, or if you leave one or more of your children out of your will, it is likely that someone will contest your will.

COMPLICATED ESTATES

If you are the beneficiary of a trust, or have any complications in your legal relationships, you may need special provisions in your will that will require the advice and services of an attorney.

BLIND OR UNABLE TO WRITE

A person who is blind, or who can only sign with an "X," should also consult a lawyer about the proper way to make and execute a will.

ESTATES OVER UNIFIED CREDIT

If you expect to have an estate that is greater than the federal unified credit (see the section on "Estate and Inheritance Taxes" in Chapter 1), you may want to consult with a CPA or tax attorney regarding tax consequences.

CONDITIONS   If you wish to put some sort of conditions or restrictions on the property you leave, you should consult a lawyer. For example, if you want to leave money to your brother only if he quits smoking, or to a hospital only if they name a wing in your honor, you should consult an attorney to be sure that your conditions are valid and can be enforced.

MAKING A SIMPLE WILL 3

Three important matters involved in making a will are:

1. identifying the people or organizations to get your property;

2. describing the property; and,

3. signing the will in a legally correct manner.

In this chapter we will be primarily concerned with the first two items. Other matters will also be discussed here, such as designating a personal representative, guardians and conservators, and funeral arrangements. Signing procedures will be discussed in Chapter 4.

IDENTIFYING BENEFICIARIES

PEOPLE When making your will, it is important to clearly identify the persons you name as your beneficiaries. In some families, names differ only by middle initial, or by the designations "Jr." and "Sr." Be sure to check everyone's name before making your will. You can also add your relationship to the beneficiary, such as "my son, John Grover Smith, Jr.," or "my niece, Dorothy Jean Parker." There could be a problem if you just listed "John Smith," and you had both an uncle named John C. Smith and a nephew named John R. Smith.

CHARITIES AND OTHER ORGANIZATIONS

The same applies to charities and other organizations. You need to give the full legal name of the organization. For example, if you gave $10,000 to "the cancer society," a problem could arise if there are three organizations, one called "The Michigan Cancer Society, Inc.," one called "The American Cancer Society of Michigan, Inc.," and one called "American Foundation for Cancer Research." If you have any doubts, call the organization and ask them for its full legal name.

Also, many charities will provide you with the language to put in your will to make a gift to it. However, if you are planning to leave a majority, or all, of your estate to a charity, and disinherit descendents, you should consult an attorney.

SPOUSE AND CHILDREN

You should mention your spouse and children in your will, even if you do not leave them anything. This will show that you are of sound mind and know who your heirs are. As mentioned in the previous chapter, if you plan to leave your spouse less than he or she would be entitled to under the elective share statute, or leave any children less than they would be entitled to under Michigan law if you did not have a will, you should consult an attorney.

REAL PROPERTY

Real estate must also be adequately described, although in most situations the street address will be sufficient. If there is any possibility of confusion, you may want to put the legal description in your will (this can be obtained from the deed or mortgage).

PERSONAL PROPERTY

HANDWRITTEN LIST OF PERSONAL PROPERTY

Because people acquire and dispose of personal property so often, it is not advisable to list personal property items in your will. Michigan law allows you to include a handwritten or signed list with your will. This will divide your personal property if the list is referred to in the will. All of the will forms in this book contain a clause stating that you may leave such a list. The list must either be in your handwriting or signed by you. It does not need to be witnessed, and can be changed at any time. (Mich. Comp. Laws Ann., Sec. 700.2513 and Mich. Stat. Ann., Sec. 27.12513.)

DESCRIBING PERSONAL PROPERTY

The list must describe the items with reasonable certainty.

Example: Do not give someone "the gold watch I received on my fiftieth birthday" if you have two gold watches. At the time of your death no one may know which watch is the one you received for your fiftieth birthday.

TYPES OF PERSONAL PROPERTY

Leaving such a list only applies to "tangible personal property" such as watches, photos, cars, furniture, jewelry, etc. It specifically does not include "money, evidence of indebtedness, documents of title, securities, and property used in a trade or business." Therefore, if you have any of these types of property they will have to be listed in your will itself.

Just be sure that your list is kept with your will. Such a list is a specific bequest, therefore be sure to read the following section.

SPECIFIC BEQUESTS

Occasionally a person will want to leave a little something to a friend or charity and the rest to the family. This can be done with a *specific bequest* such as "$1,000 to my dear friend Martha Jones." Of course there could be a problem if, at the time of death, there wasn't anything left in the estate after the specific bequests.

Example: At the time of making his will, Todd had $1,000,000 in assets. He felt generous, so he left $50,000 to a local hospital, $50,000 to a local group that takes care of homeless animals, and gave the rest to his children.

Unfortunately, several years later the stock market crashes and Todd commits suicide by jumping off a bridge. His estate at the time of his death is only worth $110,000, so after the specific bequests to the hospital and the animal shelter, and paying funeral expenses and the legal fees and expenses of probate, there was nothing left for his five children.

Another problem with specific bequests is that some of the property may be worth considerably more or less at death than when the will was made.

Example: Joe wanted his two children to share equally in his estate, and in his will he left his son $500,000 worth of stocks and his daughter $500,000 in cash. At the time of Joe's death the stock was only worth $100,000.

He should have left "fifty percent" of his estate to each child. If giving certain things to certain people is an important part of your estate plan, you can give specific items to specific persons, but remember that you may need to make a new will or a codicil if your assets change, or if their value changes significantly.

CHARITIES AND OTHER ORGANIZATIONS
As the example on page 25-26 show, it may be better to leave a charity or other organization a percentage of the residue of your estate, rather than make a specific bequest of a dollar amount or a particular item or property. See the following section on the Remainder Clause for more information about how to do this.

JOINT BENEFICIARIES
Be careful about leaving one item of personal property to more than one person. For example, if you leave something to your son and his wife, what would happen if they divorce? Even if you leave something to two of your own children, what if they can not agree about who will have possession of it? Whenever possible, leave any single item of property to one person.

REMAINDER CLAUSE

One of the most important clauses in a will is the *remainder clause*. This is the clause that says something like "all the rest, residue, and remainder of my property I leave to…" This clause is designed to make sure that the will disposes of all property owned at the time of death, and that nothing is forgotten.

In a simple will, the best way to distribute property is to put it all in the remainder clause. In the first example in the previous section, Todd's problem would have been avoided if his will had read as follows: "The rest, residue, and remainder of my estate I leave as follows: five percent to ABC Hospital, Inc.; five percent to the XYZ Animal Welfare League; and ninety percent to be divided equally among my children, D, E, F, G, and H." This would have at least ensured that his children got something and would not be left out in favor of the two charitable gifts.

ALTERNATE BENEFICIARIES

You should always provide for an *alternate beneficiary* in case the first beneficiary you name dies before you do, and you do not have a chance to make out a new will. In naming an alternate beneficiary, a couple of choices must be made.

SURVIVOR OR DESCENDANTS

Suppose your will leaves your property to your sister and brother, but your brother dies before you. Would you want your brother's share to go to your sister, or to your brother's children and grandchildren?

If you are giving property to two or more persons and you want it all to go to the other if one of them dies, then you would specify "or the survivor of them."

If, on the other hand, you want the property to go to the children of the deceased person, you should state in your will, "or their lineal descendants." This would include his or her children and grandchildren.

FAMILY OR
PERSON

If you decide you want the property to go to the children of the deceased person, you must next decide if an equal share should go to each family or to each person.

Example: Your brother dies before you, leaving three grandchildren. One is the only child of his deceased daughter, and the other two are children of his deceased son. Should all three grandchildren get equal shares, or should they take what their parent would have received?

When you want each *family* to get an equal share, it is called *per stirpes* distribution. When you want each *person* to get an equal share, it is called *per capita* distribution. Most of the wills in this book use per stirpes because that is the most common way property is left. If you wish to leave your property per capita, then you can rewrite the will substituting the words "per capita" for the words "per stirpes."

Example: Alice leaves her property to "my two daughters, Mary and Pat, in equal shares, or to their lineal descendants per stirpes." Both daughters die before Alice. Mary leaves one child, Pat leaves two children. In this case Mary's child would get one-half of the estate and Pat's children would split the other one-half of the estate (i.e., Mary's child gets one-half of the total, and Pat's children each get one-fourth). If Alice had specified per capita instead of per stirpes, then each of the three grandchildren would have gotten one-third of the total estate.

The following are diagrams of this example:

PER STIRPES DISTRIBUTION

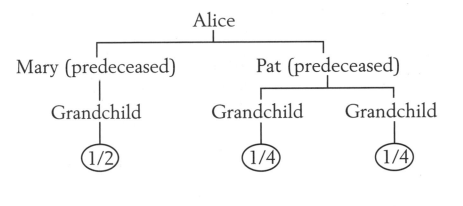

PER CAPITA DISTRIBUTION

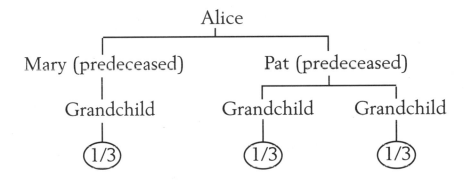

If this is still confusing to you, consider seeking the advice of an attorney.

SURVIVORSHIP CLAUSE

Many people put a *survivorship clause* in their will, stating that anyone receiving property under the will must survive for thirty days (or forty-five, sixty, etc.) after their death. This is so that if the two people die in the same accident, there will not be two probates, and the property will not go to the other party's heirs.

Example: Fred and Wilma were married and each had children by previous marriages. They did not have survivorship clauses in their wills and they were in an airplane crash. Fred's children hired several expert witnesses and a large law firm to prove that at the time of the crash Fred lived for a few minutes longer than Wilma. That way when Wilma died first, all of her property went to Fred. When he died a few minutes later, all of Fred and Wilma's property went to his children. Wilma's children got nothing.

GUARDIANS AND CONSERVATORS

If you have minor children you should name a *guardian* and a *conservator* for them. A guardian is the person who decides where the children will live and makes the other parental decisions for them. A conservator is in charge of the minor's property and inheritance. In most cases one person is appointed both guardian and conservator, but some people prefer the children to live with one person (whom they believe to have better parenting skills) and have the property held and managed by another person (whom they believe to be a better financial manager).

Example: Sandra was a widow with a young daughter. She knew that if anything happened to her, her sister would be the best person to raise her daughter. But her sister was never good with money, so when Sandra made out her will, she named her sister guardian of her daughter and her father conservator of her daughter's estate.

When naming a guardian or conservator it is always advisable to name alternates in case your first choice is unable to serve for any reason. You should also check with the intended guardian and conservator to be sure he or she is willing to take on this responsibility.

CHILDREN'S TRUST

When a child's property is held by a conservator, the conservatorship ends when the child reaches the age of eighteen, and all of the property is turned over to the child at that time. Most parents do not believe their children are competent to handle large sums of money at the age of eighteen, and prefer that the money be held until the child is twenty-one, twenty-five, thirty, or even older.

If you wish to set up a complicated system of determining when your children should receive various amounts of your estate, or if you want the property held to a higher age than thirty-five, you should consult an attorney to prepare a trust. However, if you want a simple provision that the funds be held until they reach a higher age than eighteen, and you have someone you trust to make decisions about paying for food, clothing, housing, education, and other expenses for your child, you can put that provision in your will as a children's trust.

The children's trust trustee can be the same person as the guardian or a different person. It is advisable to name an alternate trustee in case your first choice is unable to serve. Also, be sure to discuss this with your intended trustee and alternate so that you are sure they will be willing to accept this responsibility.

PERSONAL REPRESENTATIVES

A *personal representative* is the person who will be in charge of your probate. He or she will gather your assets, handle the sale of them if necessary, prepare an inventory, hire an attorney, and distribute the property. This should be a person you trust, in which case you can state in your will that no bond will be required to be posted by him or her. Otherwise the court will require that a surety bond be obtained (paid for by your estate) to guaranty the personal representative is honest.

It is best to have a Michigan resident as a personal representative because it is easier and because a bond may be required of a non-resident even if your will waives it. You can also name an alternate personal representative, just in case your first choice is unable or unwilling to serve in this capacity.

Some people like to name two persons as personal representatives in order to avoid jealousy between them, to have them check on each other's honesty, or for other reasons. However, this is not a good idea. It makes double work in getting the papers signed, and there can be problems if they cannot agree on something.

WITNESSES

A will must be witnessed by two persons to be valid in Michigan. You will notice that all of the will forms in Appendix C have spaces for the signatures of two witnesses.

Although it is not advisable, Michigan does permit a will without witnesses, but only "if it is dated, if the signature appears at the end of the will and the material provisions are in the handwriting of the testator." Such a handwritten will is called a *holographic* will. (Mich. Comp. Laws Ann., Sec. 700.2502 and Mich, Stat, Ann., Sec 700.12502.)

SELF-PROVING AFFIDAVITS

A *self-proving affidavit* is simply a notarized statement verifying the signatures of the testator and witnesses to a will. Although a will only needs two witnesses to be legal, if it also has a SELF-PROVING AFFIDAVIT it can be admitted to probate quickly and there is no need to contact witnesses. If it does not have a SELF-PROVING AFFIDAVIT, then one of the witnesses will be required to sign a statement that the will is genuine. This can delay probate if it becomes necessary to track down a witness, or if neither witness can be located (there are procedures to cover the situation where neither witness is available). There is a SELF-PROVING AFFIDAVIT for a will in Appendix C. (see form 18, p.125.) There is also a SELF-PROVING AFFIDAVIT FOR A CODICIL to a will. (see form 20. p.129.) Form 23 is a SELF-PROVING WILL PAGE to be used if you previously executed a will without a SELF-PROVING AFFIDAVIT, and would now like to add one. (see form 23, p.135.)

In an emergency situation, for example, if you are bedridden and there is no notary available, you can execute your will or CODICIL without the SELF-PROVING AFFIDAVIT. As long as it has the signature of two witnesses it will be valid. The only drawback is that at least one of the witnesses will have to sign an oath when it comes time to probate the will.

DISINHERITING SOMEONE

If you decide not to leave someone at least what they would be entitled to receive if you died without a will, you are said to be *disinheriting* that person. As we discussed earlier, you cannot disinherit a spouse because of the elective share statutes that guarantee a spouse a minimum amount of property. However, you can disinherit other relatives. For purposes of our discussion we will use the example of a child, but it could also apply to grandchildren, parents, brothers and sisters, nieces and nephews, etc. Disinheriting someone will increase the likelihood of your will being challenged in court, therefore you should see an attorney if you intend to disinherit someone.

Common reasons for a parent disinheriting a child include having already made a gift to the child, recognizing that the child is financially well off and therefore is less in need than the other children, and various events that lead to a lack of affection between the parent and child. The exact language to use in a will to disinherit someone may vary with the reason. The following discussion will give you an idea of some of the potential problems involved.

First, you should not simply leave a child out of your will. One way in which a will can be challenged is if it can be shown that the testator did not know who his or her natural heirs were. This supports a contention that the testator was not of sound mind when the will was executed. Therefore, you need to mention someone, even if you are leaving him or her nothing.

If you do leave more to one child than to another, your safest bet is to simply state what you are giving to each.

Example: "To my son, Alan, I give two-thirds of the residue of my estate. To my son, Robert, I give one-third of the residue of my estate."

If you do not leave anything to a child, you can simply state that fact.

Example: "To my son, James, I leave nothing."

In some situations, it may not be advisable to state your reasons, as this may help the disinherited person challenge the will.

Example: If you say "To my son, James, I leave nothing as he is already well provided for," and James loses his fortune before you die, then James has a basis for challenging the will by arguing that you would have left him more if you had known of his financial situation.

On the other hand, if your reason for leaving less or nothing to a child is that you made a substantial gift to that child, it may be a good idea for you to say so in your will.

Example: "To my son, Charles, I leave nothing as I have already made a gift to Charles of the family vacation home at Houghton Lake."

This makes it clear that your intention was to give Charles his share of his inheritance in advance of your death, and that the balance of your estate should go to the other children. Again, it is suggested that you seek the advice of an attorney to be sure you use the proper language for your particular situation.

FUNERAL ARRANGEMENTS

There is no harm in stating your funeral arrangement preferences in your will, but such directions are not legally enforceable, and many times a will is not found until after the funeral. Therefore it is better to tell your family of your wishes, or to make prior arrangements yourself.

MISCELLANEOUS CONSIDERATIONS

Your will can be typed, handwritten, or filled in on a form. It should have no "white-outs" or erasures. If, for some reason, it is impossible to make a will without corrections, the corrections should be initialed by you and both witnesses. If there are two or more pages, they should be fastened together and each page should be initialed by you.

NOTE: *If you use the* MICHIGAN STATUTORY WILL, *you do not need to initial each page. (see form 3, p.91.)*

FORMS

There are several different forms included in this book for easy use. You can either tear them out, photocopy them, or retype them on plain paper. The forms are self-explanatory. Just fill in the blanks with the appropriate information to fit your situation and desires. The following information may also be helpful.

MICHIGAN STATUTORY WILL

The Michigan statutes now include a MICHIGAN STATUTORY WILL for a simple will. (see form 3, p.91.) You need to be aware that this form is limited in what it can do. The MICHIGAN STATUTORY WILL (form 3) only gives you the following options:

1. to make two specific bequests.

2.   to leave your personal and household items to your spouse or children.

3.   to leave the balance of your estate, or your entire estate, to either:

- those persons who would get it if you did not have a will,

or

- one-half to those who would get it if you had no will, and one-half to your spouse's heirs if your spouse died with no will.

4.   to appoint a personal representative for your estate, and appoint a guardian and conservator for your minor children.

If you want to do anything else, you cannot use the MICHIGAN STATUTORY WILL form. For example, you cannot give 60% of your estate to one child and 40% to the other child. It would be a good idea for you to read through this form even if you do not use it, because it explains some important considerations and legal requirements which apply to any will form.

OTHER WILL FORMS

See the beginning of Appendix C for a list of the various forms and a summary of what each one provides. You will need to select the form to fit your desires as to the number and type of beneficiaries. Be sure to check Appendix B for examples of some of the forms completed for fictional people.

If you find you have a special situation that requires forms not included in the appendix, refer to the section entitled "Legal Research" in Chapter 1. If your situation is complex, and especially if your estate will exceed the federal unified credit (see the section on "Estate and Inheritance Taxes" in Chapter 1), consult an attorney.

Executing a Will

The signing of a will is a serious legal event, and must be done properly or the will may be declared invalid. Preferably, it should be done in a private room without distraction.

To be legal in Michigan, a will must be signed by the person making the will (the *testator*), and by two competent witnesses. *Competent* means they would be legally qualified to be a witness in court. Witnesses should be eighteen years of age or older, and mentally competent.

A person who is a beneficiary in the will should *not* sign as a witness. If a person named as a beneficiary in the will does sign as a witness, he or she will not be able to inherit under the will. The only exceptions are where:

1. the will was signed by a third witness, who is not a beneficiary; or

2. the beneficiary/witness would be entitled to a share of the estate if there was no will (in which case he or she will get up to the amount he or she would have received if there was no will).

Signing Procedures

Although not legally required, the best way to conduct a will signing is as follows:

- All parties should watch each other sign.

- No one should leave the scene until all have signed.

- The testator and all witnesses should be able to see each other and the will.

- The testator should state, "This is my will. I have read it and understand it, and this is how I want it to read. I want you people to be my witnesses."

- Then the testator and the witnesses should watch each other sign.

There are a few general rules of which to be aware, in the event they apply to your situation.

- The testator and witnesses may sign the will in any order. However, the witnesses must still be able to testify that the testator acknowledged his or her signature to them.

- If the testator is unable to sign his or her name to the will, he or she may direct someone else to sign. The person who signs must do so at the direction of the testator and in the testator's presence. This act of signing can either be done in the presence of the witnesses, or the witnesses can sign later if the testator makes the statement referred to above and adds, "This will was signed at my direction and in my presence." The witnesses may then sign.

- The testator and witnesses do not need to sign in each other's presence (although this would be the preferable way). The testator may sign the will in advance, and later present it to the witness and make the statement referred to above and add, "I have signed this as my will." The witnesses may then sign.

SELF-PROVING AFFIDAVITS

As explained in the last chapter, it is important to attach a SELF-PROVING AFFIDAVIT to your will. This means that you will need to have a *notary public* present to watch you and the witnesses sign. If it is impossible to have a notary present, your will is still valid, but the probate process may be delayed.

After your witnesses have signed as attesting witnesses under your name on the will, you and they should sign the self-proving page and the notary should notarize it. The notary should not be one of your witnesses.

COPIES OF YOUR WILL

It is a good idea to make at least one copy of your will, but you should not sign or notarize any copies. The reason for this is that if you cancel or intentionally destroy your original will, someone might bring out a copy and say that it is the original, or that it is a copy of a still-valid will.

AFTER SIGNING YOUR WILL 5

After you have executed your will, you may want to know where to keep your will, and what to do if you later want to cancel it or change it. These matters will be discussed in this chapter.

STORING YOUR WILL

Your will should be kept in a place safe from fire, and easily accessible to your heirs. Your personal representative should know of its whereabouts. It can be kept in a home safe or fire box, or in a safe deposit box in a bank. In some states, a will should not be placed in a safe deposit box because they are sealed at death. However, in Michigan it is easy to get a will out of a deceased person's safe deposit box.

Wills are not usually filed anywhere until after a person's death. However, for a small fee, a will may be filed with your county's probate court for safekeeping. No one has to know what you have put in your will while you are alive. Often an attorney who prepares a will offers to keep it in his or her safe deposit box at no charge. This way the attorney will likely be contacted at the time of death and will be in a good position to do the probate work.

If you are close to your children and can trust them explicitly, then you could allow one of them to keep your will in his or her safe deposit box. However, if you later decide to limit that child's share, there could be a problem.

Example: Diane made out her will, giving her property to her two children equally, and gave the will to her older child, Bill, to hold. Years later, Bill moved away and had little further contact with his mother. Diane's younger child, Mary, took care of her during her final illness, so Diane made a new will giving most of her property to Mary. Upon Diane's death, Bill returned and found the new will in Diane's house. He destroyed the new will and probated the old will, which gave him one-half of the property.

REVOKING YOUR WILL

A person who has made a will may cancel, or *revoke*, it; or may direct someone else to revoke it in his or her presence. This may be done by burning, tearing, defacing, obliterating, or destroying it with the intention and for the purpose of revoking it. Revoking one will does not reinstate, or *revive*, an older will. Ideally, the original will, and all copies, should be totally destroyed. However, if a subsequent will that only revoked part of a previous will is later revoked itself (by a revocation act rather than a declaration in writing), the revoked part of the previous will is revived. This is true unless the circumstances of the revocation of the subsequent will or subsequent declarations show no intent for the revoked part of the old will to be revived. (Mich. Comp. Laws Ann., Sec. 700.2509 and Mich. Stat. Ann., Sec. 27.12509.)

Example: Ralph tells his son, Clyde, to go to the basement safe and tear up his (Ralph's) will. If Clyde does not tear it up in Ralph's presence it is probably not effectively revoked.

A will is also revoked by the execution of a new will. The new will should contain the phrase, "I revoke any prior wills and codicils."

CHANGING YOUR WILL

You may not make any changes on your will after it has been signed. If you cross out a person's name or add a new clause to a will that has already been signed, your change will not be valid, and your entire will might become invalid.

If you wish to change some provision of your will, you can do it by executing a document called a *codicil*. A person may make an unlimited number of codicils to a will, but each one must be executed with the same formality of a will (i.e., two witnesses, etc.). Also, if there are several codicils, it can be difficult to locate all of them, figure out exactly how each one modifies the will or a previous codicil, track down the necessary witnesses, and determine how the estate is to be divided. Therefore, it is usually better to prepare a new will instead of a CODICIL.

Form 19 in Appendix C is a CODICIL. You should also use the SELF-PROVED CODICIL AFFIDAVIT and attach it to your codicil. (see form 20, p.129.) (See Chapter 3 for more information on self-proving affidavits.)

How to Make a Living Will 6

A *living will* is a document by which a person declares that he or she does not want certain types of medical treatment if he or she becomes terminally ill. A living will has nothing to do with the traditional will that distributes property.

Modern science can often keep a body alive even if the brain is permanently dead. The living will is designed for a person to be able to state in advance that he or she does not want such treatment.

In 1990, Michigan passed a law that allows a person to designate a *patient advocate*. (Mich. Comp. Laws Ann., Secs. 700.5506 through 700.5512 and Mich. Stat. Ann., Secs. 27.15506 through 27.15512.) This law is different from a traditional living will, in that a living will was only a statement of your desires concerning the use of life-prolonging procedures in the event you were terminally ill. (It did not involve appointing anyone to make decisions for you, and did not cover medical decisions or treatment where there was no terminal illness or condition).

The current Michigan law allows you to designate someone to make health care decisions for you whenever you are unable to do so for your self (even if there is no terminal condition). In other states this may be referred to as a *health care power of attorney*. The person you designate is called a *patient advocate*. Under this law, a DESIGNATION OF PATIENT

ADVOCATE AND LIVING WILL document can be signed at any time by someone who is at least eighteen years of age and of sound mind. (see form 21, p.131.)

Not anyone can be a witness to your DESIGNATION OF PATIENT ADVOCATE AND LIVING WILL, which must be signed in front of two witnesses, neither of whom are:

1. the person's spouse, parent, child, grandchild, brother, or sister;

2. the person's presumptive heir (i.e., one who will inherit from the person), or a known devisee under the person's will at the time of witnessing;

3. the person's physician;

4. the person's designated patient advocate;

5. an employee of a life or health insurance provider for the person;

6. an employee of a health facility treating the person; or

7. an employee of a home for the aged where the person lives.

The DESIGNATION OF PATIENT ADVOCATE AND LIVING WILL may include a statement of the person's desires about his or her care, custody, and medical treatment, and may specifically designate or limit the powers of the patient advocate. A patient advocate may not decide to withhold or withdraw treatment that would allow you to die, unless you specifically give him or her that power. You may also designate an alternate patient advocate in the event your first choice is unable or unwilling to act.

Before acting, the patient advocate must accept the responsibility by signing an acceptance provision (which is also included in form 21 in Appendix C).

The law creating this is fairly detailed, taking up five pages in the statutes. It covers various possible situations, such as:

- what and who determines that the patient is unable to participate in decision-making, so as to allow the patient advocate to make decisions,

- restrictions if the patient is pregnant, and

- when and under what circumstances certain types of decisions may be made.

If you have any questions about this, it is strongly suggested that you read the entire statute before you sign a DESIGNATION OF PATIENT ADVOCATE AND LIVING WILL. (Mich. Comp. Laws Ann., Secs. 700.5506 through 700.5512 and Mich. Stat. Ann., Secs. 27.15506 through 27.15512.)

An example of a completed DESIGNATION OF PATIENT ADVOCATE AND LIVING WILL (form 21) is also included in Appendix B.

How to Make Anatomical Gifts 7

The Uniform Anatomical Gift Act allows Michigan residents to donate their bodies or organs for research or transplantation. (Mich. Comp. Laws Ann., Sec. 333.10101 and Mich. Stat. Ann., Sec. 14.15(10101).) Consent may also be given by certain relatives of a deceased person but, because relatives are often in shock and too upset to make such a decision, or don't believe in body or organ donation, it is better to have your intent made clear before death. This can be done by a statement in a regular will, or by another signed document such as the UNIFORM DONOR CARD (see form 22, p.133.). The gift may be of all or part of one's body, and it may be made to a specific person such as a physician or an ill relative.

The document making the donation must be signed before two witnesses, who must also sign in each other's presence. If the donor cannot sign, then the document may be signed for him at his direction in the presence of the witnesses.

The donor may designate in the document who the physician is who will carry out the procedure.

If the document has been delivered to a specific donee, it may be amended or revoked by a person in the following ways:

- by executing and delivering a signed statement to the donee;

- by an oral statement to two witnesses and communicated to the donee;

- by an oral statement during a terminal illness or injury made to an attending physician and communicated to the donee; or

- by a signed document found on the person of the donor or in his or her effects.

If a document of gift has not been delivered to a donee, it may be revoked by any of the above methods or by destruction, cancellation, or mutilation of the document and all copies. If included in a will, it may also be revoked in the same method a will is revoked as described in Chapter 5.

GLOSSARY

A

administrator (administratrix if female). *See* personal representative.

affidavit. A written statement signed under oath before a notary public or other person authorized by law to administer oaths.

anatomical gift. The donation, upon death, of the entire body or any body part, such as the heart, liver, eyes, for the purpose of transplant, or medical research or study.

ancillary administration. The probate of assets in a state other than the decedent's primary state of residence.

B

beneficiary. A person who is entitled to receive property from a person who died (regardless of whether there is a will).

bequest. Personal property left to someone in a will.

C

codicil. A change or amendment to a will.

conservator. A person given the legal authority to manage another's financial affairs.

D

decedent. A person who has died.

descendant. A child, grandchild, great-grandchild, etc.

devise. Real property left to someone in a will. A person who is entitled to a devise is called a *devisee.*

dower rights. Certain legal rights, provided for by statute, that a wife has in her husband's property upon his death.

E

elective share. The portion of the estate which may be taken by a surviving spouse, regardless of what the will says.

escheat. The transfer of the property of a decedent to the state, when there is no other person or entity designated to receive it.

executor (executrix if female). *See* personal representative.

exempt property. Property that is exempt from distribution as a normal part of the estate.

F

family allowance. An amount of money set aside from the estate to support the family of the decedent for a period of time.

forced share. See *elective share.*

G

guardian. A person given the legal authority to manage another's non-financial affairs..

H

health care power of attorney. A power of attorney that gives the agent the authority to make decisions about the principal's health care in the event the principal is not able to make or communicate such decisions.

heir. A person who will inherit from a decedent who died without a will.

holographic will. A will that is entirely handwritten by the testator.

homestead allowance. A provision in Michigan law that allows a decedent's spouse, or minor or dependent children, to receive a certain amount from the estate in order maintain a place to live.

I

inter vivos trust. A trust created while the maker is alive.

intestate. Without making a will. One who dies without a will is said to have *died intestate.*

intestate share. The portion of the estate a spouse is entitled to receive if there is no will. In Michigan, this portion varies from one-half to all of the estate, depending upon whether the decedent had any children.

intestate succession. The manner in which a decedent's estate is distributed in the event the decedent did not have a will.

J

joint tenancy. A type of property ownership by two or more persons, in which if one owner dies, that owner's interest goes to the other joint tenants (not to the deceased owner's heirs as in tenancy in common).

L

law of intestate succession. The law which determines who is entitled to a decedent's property when there is no will.

legacy. Real property left to someone in a will. A person who is entitled to a legacy is called a *legatee.*

life estate. An estate in land that is limited to the life of the person occupying the land, or the life of another person.

life-prolonging procedures. Medical procedures and treatments designed to artificially prolong life.

living trust. *See* inter vivos trust.

living will. A document expressing the writer's desires regarding how medical care is to be handled in the event the writer is not able to express his or her wishes concerning the use of life-prolonging medical procedures.

P

patient advocate. The term used in Michigan for an agent authorized to make health care decisions.

per capita. The method of dividing an estate whereby each member of a class or group of heirs takes an equal share.

per stirpes. The method of dividing an estate whereby a class or group of heirs take the share which their deceased ancestor would have been entitled to receive.

personal representative. A person appointed by the court, or will, to oversee distribution of the property of the person who died. This is a more modern term than "administrator," "executor," etc., and applies regardless of whether there is a will.

petition for probate. The legal document that is filed with the Probate Court to begin the probate process.

probate. The process of settling a decedent's estate through the probate court.

probate estate. Assets that are subject to probate (this does not include assets which pass directly such as those owned jointly with survivorship rights, and life insurance).

R

remainder. The balance of a decedent's estate after all specific bequests are considered.

residue. *See* remainder.

revival. The reinstating of an older will, after a newer will is revoked.

S

self-proving will affidavit. An affidavit which is used to authenticate the signatures of a testator and witnesses to a will.

specific bequest or **specific devise**. A gift in a will of a specific item of property, or a specific amount of cash.

survivorship clause. A provision in the law, or in a will, that an heir must live a certain length of time after the decedent's death in order to receive property.

T

tenancy by the entireties. A type of property ownership by a married couple. This is generally the same as joint tenancy, except that it is only between a husband and wife.

tenancy in common. Ownership of property by two of more people, in which each owner's share would descend to that owner's heirs (not to the other owners as in joint tenancy).

testamentary trust. A trust that is created in a will.

testate. With a will. One who dies with a will is said to have "died testate."

testator. (**testatrix** if female.) A person who makes his or her will.

Totten trust. A trust created when a person deposits his or her own money in his or her own name, as trustee for another.

APPENDIX A
MICHIGAN COMPILED LAWS
ANNOTATED

This appendix contains portions of the Michigan laws relating to wills and probate. The primary citations in bold face are to the Michigan Compiled Laws Annotated (Mich. Comp. Laws Ann.), although the corresponding citation to the Michigan Statutes Annotated (Mich. Stat. Ann.) is also provided in brackets, [   ]. The Michigan Statutes Annotated are being phased-out, and their corresponding numbers are no longer being assigned to new legislation. The Michigan Statutes Annotated references are provided here, in the event that is the only set of Michigan laws you have available.

Michigan Compiled Laws Annotated

Sec. 558.1 Right of widow to dower. [Mich. Stat. Ann., Sec. 26.221]. The widow of every deceased person, shall be entitled to dower, or the use during her natural life, of 1/3 part of all the lands whereof her husband was seized of an estate of inheritance, at any time during the marriage, unless she is lawfully barred thereof.

Sec. 558.2 Dower in lands exchanged; election. [Mich. Stat. Ann., Sec. 26.222]. If a husband seized of an estate of inheritance in lands, exchange them for other lands, his widow shall not have dower of both, but shall make her election to be endowed of the lands given, or of those taken in exchange; and if such election be not evinced by the commencement of proceedings to recover her dower of the lands given in exchange, within 1 year after the death of her husband, she shall be deemed to have elected to take her dower of the lands received in exchange.

Sec. 558.3 Dower in mortgaged lands; mortgage before marriage. [Mich. Stat. Ann., Sec. 26.223]. When a person seized of an estate of inheritance in lands, shall have executed a mortgage of such estate before marriage, his widow shall be entitled to a dower out of the lands mortgaged, as against every person except the mortgagee and those claiming under him.

Sec. 558.4 Dower in mortgaged lands; purchase money mortgage given after marriage. [Mich. Stat. Ann., Sec. 26.224]. When a husband shall purchase lands during coverture, and shall at the same time mortgage his estate in such lands to secure the payment of the purchase money, his widow shall not be entitled to dower out of such lands, as against the mortgagee or those claiming under him, although she shall not have united in such mortgage, but she shall be entitled to her dower as against all other persons.

Sec. 558.5 Dower in surplus of proceeds from foreclosure of mortgage. [Mich. Stat. Ann., Sec. 26.225]. Where in either of the cases mentioned in the 2 last preceding sections, or in case of a mortgage in which she shall have joined with her husband, the mortgagee, or those claiming under him shall after the death of the husband cause the mortgaged premises to be sold by virtue of such mortgage, and any surplus shall remain after payment of the moneys due thereon and the costs and charges of the sale, such widow shall be entitled to the interest or income of 1/3 part of such surplus, for her life, as dower.

Sec. 558.6 Dower in lands released by payment of mortgage. [Mich. Stat. Ann., Sec. 26.226]. If, in either of the cases above specified, the heir or other person claiming under the husband, shall pay and satisfy the mortgage, the amount so paid shall be deducted from the value of the land, and the widow shall have set out to her, for her dower in the mortgaged lands, the value of 1/3 of the residue after such deduction.

Sec. 558.7 Dower in aliened lands; estimation. [Mich. Stat. Ann., Sec. 26.227]. When a widow shall be entitled to dower out of any lands which shall have been aliened by the husband in his lifetime, and such lands shall have been enhanced in value after the alienation, such lands shall be estimated, in setting out the widow's dower, according to their value at the time when they were so aliened.

Sec. 558.12 Alternative dower rights before assignment; occupation, profits and rents receipts. [Mich. Stat. Ann., Sec. 26.228]. When a widow is entitled to dower in the lands of which her husband died seized, she may continue to occupy the same with the children or other heirs of the deceased, or may receive 1/3 part of the rents, issues and profits thereof, so long as the heirs or others interested do not object, without having the dower assigned.

Sec. 558.13 Barring of dower; joining in conveyance, release. [Mich. Stat. Ann., Sec. 26.229]. A married woman residing within this state may bar her right of dower in any estate conveyed by her husband or by his guardian, if he be under guardianship, by joining in the deed of conveyance and acknowledging the same as prescribed in the preceding chapter, or by joining with her husband in a subsequent deed, acknowledged in like manner; or by deed executed by the wife alone to one who has theretofore acquired and then holds the husband's title, provided the intent to bar her right of dower shall be expressed in said deed.

Sec. 558.14 Barring of dower; jointure. [Mich. Stat. Ann., Sec. 26.230]. A woman may also be barred of her dower in all the lands of her husband by a jointure settled on her with her assent before the marriage, provided such jointure consists of a freehold estate in lands for the life of the wife at least, to take effect in possession or profit immediately on the death of the husband.

Sec. 558.15 Barring of dower; expression of assent to jointure. [Mich. Stat. Ann., Sec. 26.231]. Such assent shall be expressed, if the woman be of full age, by her becoming a party to the conveyance by which it is settled, and if she be under age, by her joining with her father or guardian in such conveyance.

Sec. 558.16 Barring of dower; antenuptial pecuniary provisions. [Mich. Stat. Ann., Sec. 26.232]. Any pecuniary provision that shall be made for the benefit of an intended wife, and in lieu of dower, shall, if assented to as provided in the preceding section, bar her right of dower in all the lands of her husband.

Sec. 558.20 Renewal of dower. [Mich. Stat. Ann., Sec. 26.236]. If a woman is lawfully evicted of lands assigned to her as dower, or settled upon her as jointure or is deprived of the provision made for her by will or otherwise, in lieu of dower, she may be endowed anew, in like manner as if such assignment, jointure or other provision had not been made.

Sec. 558.21 Dower right of aliens and nonresidents. [Mich. Stat. Ann., Sec. 26.237]. A woman being an alien, shall not on that account be barred of her dower, and any woman residing out of the state, shall be entitled to dower of the lands of her deceased husband, lying in this state, of which her husband died seized, and the same may be assigned to her, or recovered by her, in like manner as if she and her deceased husband had been residents within the state at the time of his death.

Sec. 558.22 Waste liability; maintenance of tenements and appurtenances. [Mich. Stat. Ann., Sec. 26.238]. No woman, who shall be endowed of any lands, shall commit or suffer any waste on the same, but every woman so endowed shall maintain the houses and tenements, with the fences and appurtenances in good repair, and shall be liable to the person having the next immediate estate of inheritance therein, for all damages occasioned by any waste committed or suffered by her.

Sec. 558.24 Damages upon recovery of dower; widow's rights. [Mich. Stat. Ann., Sec. 26.240]. Whenever in any action brought for the purpose, a widow shall recover her dower in lands of which her husband shall have died seized, she shall be entitled also to recover damages for the withholding of such dower.

Sec. 558.25 Damages upon recovery of dower; measure. [Mich. Stat. Ann., Sec. 26.241]. Such damages shall be 1/3 part of the annual value of the mesne profits of the lands in which she shall so recover her dower, to be estimated in a suit against the heirs of her husband, from the time of his death; and in suits against other persons from the time of her demanding her dower of such persons.

Sec. 558.26 Damages upon recovery of dower; use of added improvements. [Mich. Stat. Ann., Sec. 26.242]. Such damages shall not be estimated for the use of any permanent improvements made after the death of her husband by his heirs, or by any other person claiming title to such lands.

Sec. 558.27 Damages upon recovery of dower; against heir alienating land. [Mich. Stat. Ann., Sec. 26.243]. When a widow shall recover her dower in any lands alienated by the heir of her husband, she shall be entitled to recover of such heir, in an action on the case, her damages for withholding such dower, from the time of the death of her husband to the time of the alienation by the heir not exceeding 6 years in the whole; and the amount which she shall be entitled to recover from such heir, shall be deducted from the amount she would otherwise be entitled to recover from such grantee, and any amount recovered as damages, from such grantee, shall be deducted from the sum she would otherwise be entitled to recover from such heir.

Sec. 558.28 Assignment of dower; effect of acceptance. [Mich. Stat. Ann., Sec. 26.244]. When the widow shall have accepted an assignment of dower, in satisfaction of her claim upon all the lands of her husband, it shall be a bar to any further claim of dower against the heir of such husband, or any grantee of such heir, or any grantee of such husband, unless such widow shall have been lawfully evicted of the lands so assigned to her as aforesaid.

Sec. 558.29 Collusive recovery by widow; effect on rights of infants or others entitled to land. [Mich. Stat. Ann., Sec. 26.245]. When a widow not having right to dower, shall during the infancy of the heirs of the husband, or any of them, or of any person entitled to the lands, recover dower by the default or collusion of the guardian of such infant, heir or other person, such heir or other person so entitled shall not be prejudiced thereby, but when he comes of full age, he shall have an action against such widow, to recover the lands so wrongfully awarded for dower.

Sec. 700.2101 Intestate estate. [Mich. Stat. Ann., Sec. 27.12101]

(1) Any part of a decedent's estate not effectively disposed of by will passes by intestate succession to the decedent's heirs as prescribed in this act, except as modified by the decedent's will.

(2) A decedent by will may expressly exclude or limit the right of an individual or class to succeed to property of the decedent that passes by intestate succession. If that individual or a member of that class survives the decedent, the share of the decedent's intestate estate to which that individual or class would have succeeded passes as if that individual or each member of that class had disclaimed his or her intestate share.

Sec. 700.2102 Share of spouse. [Mich. Stat. Ann., Sec. 27.12102]

(1) The intestate share of a decedent's surviving spouse is 1 of the following:

(a) The entire intestate estate if no descendant or parent of the decedent survives the decedent.

(b) The first $150,000.00, plus 1/2 of any balance of the intestate, if all of the decedent's surviving descendants are also descendants of the surviving spouse and there is no other descendant of the surviving spouse who survives the decedent.

(c) The first $150,000.00, plus 3/4 of any balance of the intestate estate, if no descendant of the decedent survives the decedent, but a parent of the decedent survives the decedent.

(d) The first $150,000.00, plus 1/2 of any balance of the intestate estate, if all of the decedent's surviving descendants are also descendants of the surviving spouse and the surviving spouse has 1 or more surviving descendants who are not descendants of the decedent.

(e) The first $150,000.00, plus 1/2 of any balance of the intestate estate, if 1 or more, but not all, of the decedent's surviving descendants are not descendants of the surviving spouse.

(f) The first $100,000.00, plus 1/2 of any balance of the intestate estate, if none of the decedent's surviving descendants are descendants of the surviving spouse.

(2) Each dollar amount listed in subsection (1) shall be adjusted as provided in section 1210.

Sec. 700.2103 Share of heirs other than surviving spouse. [Mich. Stat. Ann., Sec.

27.12103] Any part of the intestate estate that does not pass to the decedent's surviving spouse under section 2102, or the entire intestate estate if there is no surviving spouse, passes in the following order to the following individuals who survive the decedent:

(a) The decedent's descendants by representation.

(b) If there is no surviving descendant, the decedent's parents equally if both survive or to the surviving parent.

(c) If there is no surviving descendant or parent, the descendants of the decedent's parents or of either of them by representation.

(d) If there is no surviving descendant, parent, or descendant of a parent, but the decedent is survived by 1 or more grandparents or descendants of grandparents, 1/2 of the estate passes to the decedent's paternal grandparents equally if both survive, or to the surviving paternal grandparent, or to the descendants of the decedent's paternal grandparents or either of them if both are deceased, the descendants taking by representation; and the other 1/2 passes to the decedent's maternal relatives in the same manner. If there is no surviving grandparent or descendant of a grandparent on either the paternal or the maternal side, the entire estate passes to the decedent's relatives on the other side in the same manner as the 1/2.

700.2104 Requirement that heir survive decedent for 120 hours. [Mich. Stat. Ann., Sec. 27.12104] An individual who fails to survive the decedent by 120 hours is considered to have predeceased the decedent for purposes of homestead allowance, exempt property, and intestate succession, and the decedent's heirs are determined accordingly. If it is not established by clear and convincing evidence that an individual who would otherwise be an heir survived the decedent by 120 hours, it is considered that the individual failed to survive for the required period. This section does not apply if its application would result in a taking of the intestate estate by the state under section 2105.

Sec. 700.2105 No taker; effect. [Mich. Stat. Ann., Sec. 27.12105] If there is no taker under the provisions of this article, the intestate estate passes to this state.

Sec. 700.2106 Representation. [Mich. Stat. Ann., Sec. 27.12106]

(1) If, under section 2103(a), a decedent's intestate estate or a part of the estate passes by representation to the decedent's descendants, the estate or part of the estate is divided into as many equal shares as the total of the surviving descendants in the generation nearest to the decedent that contains 1 or more surviving descendants and the deceased descendants in the same generation who left surviving descendants, if any. Each surviving descendant in the nearest generation is allocated 1 share. The remaining shares, if any, are combined and then divided in the same manner among the surviving descendants of the deceased descendants as if the surviving descendants who were allocated a share and their surviving descendants had predeceased the decedent.

(2) If, under section 2103(c) or (d), a decedent's intestate estate or a part of the estate passes by representation to the descendants of the decedent's deceased parents or either of them or to the descendants of the decedent's deceased paternal or maternal grandparents or either of them, the estate or part of the estate is divided into as many equal shares as the total of the surviving descendants in the generation nearest the deceased parents or either of them, or the deceased grandparents or either of them, that contains 1 or more surviving descendants and the deceased descendants in the same generation who left surviving descendants, if any. Each surviving descendant in the nearest generation is allocated 1 share. The remaining shares, if any, are combined and then divided in the same manner among the surviving descendants of the deceased descendants as if the

surviving descendants who were allocated a share and their surviving descendants had predeceased the decedent.

(3) As used in this section:

(a) "Deceased descendant," "deceased parent," or "deceased grandparent" means a descendant, parent, or grandparent who either predeceased the decedent or is considered to have predeceased the decedent under section 2104.

(b) "Surviving descendant" means a descendant who neither predeceased the decedent nor is considered to have predeceased the decedent under section 2104.

Sec. 700.2107 Relative of half blood. [Mich. Stat. Ann., Sec. 27.12107] A relative of the half blood inherits the same share he or she would inherit if he or she were of the whole blood.

Sec. 700.2108 Afterborn heirs. [Mich. Stat. Ann., Sec. 27.121-8] An individual in gestation at a particular time is treated as living at that time if the individual lives 120 hours or more after birth.

Sec. 700.2109 Advancements. [Mich. Stat. Ann., Sec. 27.12109]

(1) If an individual dies intestate as to all or a portion of his or her estate, property the decedent gave during the decedent's lifetime to an individual who, at the decedent's death, is an heir is treated as an advancement against the heir's intestate share only under either of the following circumstances:

(a) The decedent declared in a contemporaneous writing or the heir acknowledged in writing that the gift is an advancement.

(b) The decedent's contemporaneous writing or the heir's written acknowledgment otherwise indicates that the gift is to be taken into account in computing the division and distribution of the decedent's intestate estate.

(2) For purposes of subsection (1), property advanced is valued as of the time the heir came into possession or enjoyment of the property or as of the time of the decedent's death, whichever first occurs.

(3) If the recipient of property advanced fails to survive the decedent, the property is not taken into account in computing the division and distribution of the decedent's intestate estate, unless the decedent's contemporaneous writing provides otherwise.

Sec. 700.2201 Surviving spouse's right to elective share. [Mich. Stat. Ann., Sec. 27.12201] Subject to sections 2203 to 2205, upon an individual's death, the individual's surviving spouse has the right described by section 2202.

Sec. 700.2202 Election of surviving spouse. [Mich. Stat. Ann., Sec. 27.12202]

(1) The surviving widow of a decedent who was domiciled in this state and who dies intestate may file with the court an election in writing that she elects to take 1 of the following:

(a) Her intestate share under section 2102.

(b) Her dower right under sections 1 to 29 of 1846 RS 66, MCL 558.1 to 558.29.

(2) The surviving spouse of a decedent who was domiciled in this state and who dies testate may file with the court an election in writing that the spouse elects 1 of the following:

(a) That the spouse will abide by the terms of the will.

(b) That the spouse will take 1/2 of the sum or share that would have passed to the spouse had the testator died intestate, reduced by 1/2 of the value of all property derived by the spouse from the decedent by any means other than testate or intestate succession upon the decedent's death.

(c) If a widow, that she will take her dower right under sections 1 to 29 of 1846 RS 66, MCL 558.1 to 558.29.

(3) The surviving spouse electing under subsection (1) is limited to 1 choice. Unless the testator's will plainly shows a contrary intent, the surviving spouse electing under subsection (2) is limited to 1 choice. The right of election of the surviving spouse must be exercised during the lifetime of the surviving spouse. The election must be made within 63 days after the date for presentment of claims or within 63 days after service of the inventory upon the surviving spouse, whichever is later.

(4) Notice of right of election shall be served upon the decedent's spouse, if any, as provided in section 3705(5), and proof of that notice shall be filed with the court. An election as provided by this section may be filed instead of service of notice and filing of proof.

(5) In the case of a legally incapacitated person, the right of election may be exercised only by order of the court in which a proceeding as to that person's property is pending, after finding that exercise is necessary to provide adequate support for the legally incapacitated person during that person's life expectancy.

(6) The surviving spouse of a decedent who was not domiciled in this state is entitled to election against the intestate estate or against the will only as may be provided by the law of the place in which the decedent was domiciled at the time of death.

(7) As used in subsection (2), "property derived by the spouse from the decedent" includes all of the following transfers:

(a) A transfer made within 2 years before the decedent's death to the extent that the transfer is subject to federal gift or estate taxes.

(b) A transfer made before the date of death subject to a power retained by the decedent that would make the property, or a portion of the property, subject to federal estate tax.

(c) A transfer effectuated by the decedent's death through joint ownership, tenancy by the entireties, insurance beneficiary, or similar means.

Sec. 700.2205 Waiver of rights by surviving spouse. [Mich. Stat. Ann., Sec. 27.12205] The rights of the surviving spouse to a share under intestate succession, homestead allowance, election, dower, exempt property, or family allowance may be waived, wholly or partially, before or after marriage, by a written contract, agreement, or waiver signed by the party waiving after fair disclosure. Unless it provides to the contrary, a waiver of "all rights" in the property or estate of a present or prospective spouse or a complete property settlement entered into after or in anticipation of separate maintenance is a waiver of all rights to homestead allowance, election, dower, exempt property, and family allowance by the spouse in the property of the other and is an irrevocable renunciation by the spouse of all benefits that would otherwise pass to the spouse from the other spouse by intestate succession or by virtue of a will executed before the waiver or property settlement.

Sec. 700.2301 Entitlement of spouse; premarital will. [Mich. Stat. Ann., Sec. 27.12301]

(1) Except as provided in subsection

(2), if a testator's surviving spouse marries the testator after the testator executes his or her will, the surviving spouse is entitled to receive, as an intestate share, not less than the value of the share of the estate the surviving spouse would have received if the testator had died intestate as to that portion of the testator's estate, if any, that is not any of the following:

(a) Property devised to a child of the testator who was born before the testator married the surviving spouse and who is not the surviving spouse's child.

(b) Property devised to a descendant of a child described in subdivision (a).

(c) Property that passes under section 2603 or 2604 to a child described in subdivision (a) or to a descendant of such a child.

(2) Subsection (1) does not apply if any of the following are true:

(a) From the will or other evidence, it appears that the will was made in contemplation of the testator's marriage to the surviving spouse.

(b) The will expresses the intention that it is to be effective notwithstanding a subsequent marriage.

(c) The testator provided for the spouse by transfer outside the will, and the intent that the transfer be a substitute for a testamentary provision is shown by the testator's statements or is reasonably inferred from the amount of the transfer or other evidence.

(3) In satisfying the share provided by this section, devises made by the will to the testator's surviving spouse, if any, are applied first, and other devises, other than a devise to a child of the testator who was born before the testator married the surviving spouse and who is not the surviving spouse's child or a devise or substitute gift under section 2603 or 2604 to a descendant of such a child, abate as provided in section 3902.

Sec. 700.2302 Omitted children. [Mich. Stat. Ann., Sec. 27.12302]

(1) Except as provided in subsection (2), if a testator fails to provide in his or her will for a child of the testator born or adopted after the execution of the will, the omitted after-born or after-adopted child receives a share in the estate as provided in 1 of the following:

(a) If the testator had no child living when he or she executed the will, an omitted after-born or after-adopted child receives a share in the estate equal in value to that which the child would have received had the testator died intestate, unless the will devised all or substantially all of the estate to the other parent of the omitted child and that other parent survives the testator and is entitled to take under the will.

(b) If the testator had 1 or more children living when he or she executed the will, and the will devised property or an interest in property to 1 or more of the then-living children, an omitted after-born or after-adopted child is entitled to share in the testator's estate subject to all of the following:

(i) The portion of the testator's estate in which the omitted after-born or after-adopted child is entitled to share is limited to devises made to the testator's then-living children under the will.

(ii) The omitted after-born or after-adopted child is entitled to receive the share of the testator's estate, as limited in subparagraph (i), that the child would have received had the testator included all omitted after-born and after-adopted children with the children to whom devises were made under the will and had given an equal share of the estate to each child.

(iii) To the extent feasible, the interest granted an omitted after-born or after-adopted child under this section must be of the same character, whether equitable or legal, present or future, as that devised to the testator's then-living children under the will.

(iv) In satisfying a share provided by this subdivision, devises to the testator's children who were living when the will was executed abate ratably. In abating the devises of the then-living children, the court shall preserve to the maximum extent possible the character of the testamentary plan adopted by the testator.

(2) Subsection (1) does not apply if either of the following applies:

(a) It appears from the will that the omission was intentional.

(b) The testator provided for the omitted after-born or after-adopted child by transfer outside the will and the intent that the transfer be a substitute for a testamentary provision is shown by the testator's statements or is reasonably inferred from the amount of the transfer or other evidence.

(3) If at the time of execution of the will the testator fails to provide in his or her will for a living child solely because he or she believes the child to be dead, the child is entitled to share in the estate as if the child were an omitted after-born or after-adopted child.

(4) In satisfying a share provided by subsection (1)(a), devises made by the will abate under section 3902.

Sec. 700.2402 Homestead allowance. [Mich. Stat. Ann., Sec. 27.12402] A decedent's surviving spouse is entitled to a homestead allowance of $15,000.00, adjusted as provided in section 1210. If there is no surviving spouse, each minor child and each dependent child of the decedent is entitled to a homestead allowance equal to $15,000.00, adjusted as provided in section 1210, divided by the number of the decedent's minor and dependent children. The homestead allowance is exempt from and has priority over all claims against the estate, except administration costs and expenses and reasonable funeral and burial expenses. A homestead allowance is in addition to any share passing to the surviving spouse or minor or dependent child by the will of the decedent, unless otherwise provided, by intestate succession, or by elective share.

Sec. 700.2403 Family allowance. [Mich. Stat. Ann., Sec. 27.12403]

(1) For their maintenance during the period of administration, a reasonable family allowance is payable to the decedent's surviving spouse and minor children whom the decedent was obligated to support, and children of the decedent or another who were in fact being supported by the decedent, which allowance shall not continue for longer than 1 year if the estate is inadequate to discharge allowed claims. The family allowance may be paid in a lump sum or in periodic installments. The family allowance is payable to the surviving spouse, if living, for the use of the surviving spouse and minor and dependent children; otherwise to the children or persons having their care and custody. If a minor child or dependent child is not living with the surviving spouse, the allowance may be paid partially to the child or to a fiduciary or other person having the child's care and custody, and partially to the spouse, as their needs may appear.

(2) The family allowance is exempt from and has priority over all claims except administration costs and expenses, reasonable funeral and burial expenses, and the homestead allowance. The family allowance is not chargeable against a benefit or share passing to the surviving spouse or children by the will of the decedent, unless otherwise provided, by intestate succession, or by way of elective share. The death of an individual entitled to family allowance terminates the right to allowances not yet paid.

Sec. 700.2404 Exempt property. [Mich. Stat. Ann., Sec. 27.12404]

(1) The decedent's surviving spouse is also entitled to household furniture, automobiles, furnishings, appliances, and personal effects from the estate up to a value not to exceed $10,000.00 more than the amount of any security interests to which the property is subject. If there is no surviving spouse, the decedent's children are entitled jointly to the same value.

(2) If encumbered assets are selected and the value in excess of security interests, plus that of other exempt property, is less than $10,000.00, or if there is not $10,000.00 worth of exempt property in the estate, the spouse or children are entitled to other assets of the estate, if any, to the extent necessary to make up the $10,000.00 value. Rights to exempt property and assets needed to make up a deficiency of exempt property have priority over all claims against the estate, except that the right to assets to make up a deficiency of exempt property abates as necessary to permit payment of all of the following in the following order:

(a) Administration costs and expenses.

(b) Reasonable funeral and burial expenses.

(c) Homestead allowance.

(d) Family allowance.

(3) The rights under this section are in addition to a benefit or share passing to the surviving spouse or children by the decedent's will, unless otherwise provided, by intestate succession, or by elective share. The $10,000.00 amount expressed in this section shall be adjusted as provided in section 1210.

Sec. 700.2502 Execution; witnessed wills; holographic wills. [Mich. Stat. Ann., Sec. 27.12502]

(1) Except as provided in subsection (2) and in sections 2503, 2506, and 2513, a will is valid only if it is all of the following:

(a) In writing.

(b) Signed by the testator or in the testator's name by some other individual in the testator's conscious presence and by the testator's direction.

(c) Signed by at least 2 individuals, each of whom signed within a reasonable time after he or she witnessed either the signing of the will as described in subdivision (b) or the testator's acknowledgment of that signature or acknowledgment of the will.

(2) A will that does not comply with subsection (1) is valid as a holographic will, whether or not witnessed, if it is dated, and if the testator's signature and the document's material portions are in the testator's handwriting.

(3) Intent that the document constitutes a testator's will can be established by extrinsic evidence, including, for a holographic will, portions of the document that are not in the testator's handwriting.

Sec. 700.2504 Self-proved will. [Mich. Stat. Ann., Sec. 27.12504]

(1) A will may be simultaneously executed, attested, and made self-proved by acknowledgment of the will by the testator and 2 witnesses' sworn statements, each made before an officer authorized to administer oaths under the laws of the state in which execution occurs and evidenced by the officer's certificate, under official seal, in substantially the following form: {See form 18 in Appendix C}

(2) An attested will may be made self-proved at any time after its execution by the acknowledgment of the will by the testator and the sworn statements of the witnesses to the will, each made before an officer authorized to administer oaths under the laws of the state in which the acknowledgment occurs and evidenced by the officer's certificate, under the official seal, attached or annexed to the will in substantially the following form: {See form 23 in Appendix C}

(3) A codicil to a will may be simultaneously executed and attested, and both the codicil and the original will made self-proved, by acknowledgment of the codicil by the testator and by witnesses' sworn statements, each made before an officer authorized to administer oaths under the laws of the state in which execution occurs and

evidenced by the officer's certificate, under official seal, in substantially the following form: {See form 20 in Appendix C}

(4) If necessary to prove the will's due execution, a signature affixed to a self-proving sworn statement attached to a will is considered a signature affixed to the will.

(5) Instead of the testator and witnesses each making a sworn statement before an officer authorized to administer oaths as prescribed in subsections (1) to (3), a will or codicil may be made self-proved by a written statement that is not a sworn statement. This statement shall state, or incorporate by reference to an attestation clause, the facts regarding the testator and the formalities observed at the signing of the will or codicil as prescribed in subsections (1) to (3). The testator and witnesses shall sign the statement, which must include its execution date and must begin with substantially the following language: "I certify (or declare) under penalty for perjury under the law of the state of Michigan that...".

Sec. 700.2511 Testamentary additions to trusts. [Mich. Stat. Ann., Sec. 27.12511]

(1) A will may validly devise property to the trustee of a trust established or to be established in any of the following manners:

(a) During the testator's lifetime by the testator, by the testator and some other person, or by some other person, including a funded or unfunded life insurance trust, although the settlor has reserved any or all rights of ownership of the insurance contracts.

(b) At the testator's death by the testator's devise to the trustee, if the trust is identified in the testator's will and its terms are set forth in a written instrument, other than a will, executed before, concurrently with, or after the execution of the testator's will or in another individual's will if that other individual has predeceased the testator, regardless of the existence, size, or character of the trust corpus.

(2) A devise described in subsection (1) is not invalid because the trust is amendable or revocable, or because the trust was amended after the execution of the will or the testator's death. Unless the testator's will provides otherwise, property devised to a trust described in subsection (1) is not held under a testamentary trust of the testator, but it becomes a part of the trust to which it is devised, and shall be administered and disposed of in accordance with the provisions of the governing instrument setting forth the terms of the trust, including an amendment to the trust made before or after the testator's death.

(3) Unless the testator's will provides otherwise, a revocation or termination of the trust before the testator's death causes the devise to lapse.

Sec. 700.2513 Separate writing identifying devise of certain types of tangible personal property. [Mich. Stat. Ann., Sec. 27.12513] Whether or not the provisions relating to a holographic will apply, a will may refer to a written statement or list to dispose of items of tangible personal property not otherwise specifically disposed of by the will, other than money. To be admissible under this section as evidence of the intended disposition, the writing must be either in the testator's handwriting or signed by the testator at the end, and must describe the items and the devisees

with reasonable certainty. The writing may be referred to as one to be in existence at the time of the testator's death; it may be prepared before or after the execution of the will; it may be altered by the testator after its preparation; and it may be a writing that has no significance apart from its effect on the dispositions made by the will.

Sec. 700.2718 Representation; per capita at each generation; per stirpes. [Mich. Stat. Ann., Sec. 27.12718]

(1) If an applicable statute or a governing instrument calls for the property to be distributed "by representation" or "per capita at each generation," the property is divided into as many equal shares as there are surviving descendants in the generation nearest to the designated ancestor that contains 1 or more surviving descendants and deceased descendants in the same generation who left surviving descendants, if any. Each surviving descendant in the nearest generation is allocated 1 share. The remaining shares, if any, are combined and then divided in the same manner among the surviving descendants of the deceased descendants as if the surviving descendants who were allocated a share and their surviving descendants had predeceased the distribution date. This rule of construction applies to documents originally created on and after April 1, 2000, and to all instruments amended on and after April 1, 2000, that use the phrase "by representation" or "per capita at each generation." If an amendment uses either phrase, the rule of this section applies to the entire instrument.

(2) If a governing instrument calls for property to be distributed "per stirpes," the property is divided into as many equal shares as there are surviving children of the designated ancestor and deceased children who left surviving descendants. Each surviving child, if any, is allocated 1 share. The share of each deceased child with surviving descendants is divided in the same manner, with subdivision repeating at each succeeding generation until the property is fully allocated among surviving descendants.

(3) For the purposes of subsections (1) and (2), a deceased individual who left no surviving descendant is disregarded, and an individual who leaves a surviving ancestor who is a descendant of the designated ancestor is not entitled to a share.

(4) As used in this section:

(a) "Deceased child" or "deceased descendant" means a child or descendant who either predeceases the distribution date or is considered to predecease the distribution date under section 2702.

(b) "Distribution date" means, with respect to an interest, the time when the interest is to take effect in possession or enjoyment. The distribution date does not need to occur at the beginning or end of a calendar day, but can occur at a time during the course of a day.

(c) "Surviving ancestor," "surviving child," or "surviving descendant" means an ancestor, a child, or a descendant who does not predecease the distribution date and is not considered to have predeceased the distribution date under section 2702.

APPENDIX B
SAMPLE FORMS

This appendix contains examples of some of the forms from appendix B, which have been filled-in for fictional people. This should give you a better idea of how your forms should look when completed.

Where the number of pages has been filled in (e.g., "Page 2 of _7_ pages."), it has been assumed that the SELF-PROVING WILL AFFIDAVIT (form 18) has been added as the last page. However, the SELF-PROVING WILL AFFIDAVIT has not been included in each example.

The following completed forms are included in this appendix:

MICHIGAN STATUTORY WILL
NOTICE

1. An individual age 18 or older and of sound mind may sign a will.
2. There are several kinds of wills. If you choose to complete this form, you will have a Michigan statutory will. If this will does not meet your wishes in any way, you should talk with a lawyer before choosing a Michigan statutory will.
3. Warning! It is strongly recommended that you do not add or cross out any words on this form except for filling in the blanks because all or part of this will may not be valid if you do so.
4. This will has no effect on jointly held assets, on retirement plan benefits, or on life insurance on your life if you have named a beneficiary who survives you.
5. This will is not designed to reduce estate taxes.
6. This will treats adopted children and children born outside of wedlock who would inherit if their parent died without a will the same way as children born or conceived during marriage.
7. You should keep this will in your safe deposit box or other safe place. By paying a small fee, you may file this will in your county's probate court for safekeeping. You should tell your family where the will is kept.
8. You may make and sign a new will at any time. If you marry or divorce after you sign this will, you should make and sign a new will.

INSTRUCTIONS:
1. To have a Michigan statutory will, you must complete the blanks on the will form. You may do this yourself, or direct someone to do it for you. You must either sign the will or direct someone else to sign it in your name and in your presence.
2. Read the entire Michigan statutory will carefully before you begin filling in the blanks. If there is anything you do not understand, you should ask a lawyer to explain it to you.

MICHIGAN STATUTORY WILL OF

Henry Edsel Ford
(Print or type your full name)

ARTICLE 1. DECLARATIONS

This is my will and I revoke any prior wills and codicils. I live in __Wayne__ County, Michigan.

My spouse is ____Holley Dodge Ford____
(Insert spouse's name or write "None")

My children now living are:

__Fred Ford__   __Joe Louis Ford__
(Insert names or write "None")

__Ann Allen Ford Fischer__   __Smokey Robinson Ford__

__Benton Harbor Ford__

Page 1 of _7_ pages

67

ARTICLE 2. DISPOSITION OF MY ASSETS

2.1   CASH GIFTS TO PERSONS OR CHARITIES. (Optional)

I can leave no more that two (2) cash gifts. I make the following cash gifts to the persons or charities in the amounts stated here. Any transfer tax due upon my death shall be paid from the balance of my estate and not from these gifts.

Full name and address of person or charity to receive cash gift.
(Name only one (1) person or charity here)

<u>   Detroit Institute of Arts   </u>
(Insert name of person or charity)

<u>   Woodward Ave., Detroit, MI   </u>
(Insert address)

AMOUNT OF GIFT (In figures): $<u> 10,000.00   </u>

AMOUNT OF GIFT (In words): $<u>   Ten thousand   </u> Dollars

Henry Edsel Ford
(Your Signature)

Full name and address of person or charity to receive cash gift.
(Name only one (1) person or charity here)

<u>   Harry J. Bennett III   </u>
(Insert name of person or charity)

<u>   3495 Lake Shore Drive, Grosse Pointe, Farms, MI   </u>
(Insert address)

AMOUNT OF GIFT (In figures): $<u> 10,000.00   </u>

AMOUNT OF GIFT (In words): $<u>   Ten thousand   </u> Dollars

Henry Edsel Ford
(Your Signature)

2.2   PERSONAL AND HOUSEHOLD ITEMS.

I may leave a separate list or statement either in my handwriting or signed by me at the end, regarding gifts of specific books, jewelry, clothing, automobiles, furniture, and other personal and household items.

I give my spouse all my books, jewelry, clothing, automobiles, furniture, and other personal and household items not included on any such separate list or statement. If I am not married at the time I sign this will, or if my spouse dies before me, my personal representative shall distribute those items, as equally as possible, among my children who survive me. If no children survive me, these items shall be distributed as set forth in paragraph 2.3.

2.3   ALL OTHER ASSETS.

I give everything else I own to my spouse. If I am not married at the time I sign this will, or if my spouse dies before me, I give these assets to my children and the descendants of any deceased child. If no spouse, children, or descendants of children survive me, I choose one of the following distribution clauses by signing my name on the line after that clause. If I sign on both lines, or if I fail to sign on either line, or if I am not now married, these assets will go under distribution clause (b).

Distribution clause, if no spouse, children, or descendants of children survive me (Select only one).
(a)   One-half to be distributed to my heirs as if I did not have a will, and one-half to be distributed to my spouse's heirs as if my spouse had died just after me without a will.

Henry Edsel Ford
_____
(Your Signature)

(b)   All to be distributed to my heirs as if I did not have a will.

_____
(Your Signature)

ARTICLE 3. NOMINATIONS OF PERSONAL REPRESENTATIVE, GUARDIAN, AND CONSERVATOR

Personal representatives, guardians, and conservators have a great deal of responsibility. The role of a personal representative is to collect your assets, pay debts and taxes from those assets, and distribute the remaining assets as directed in the will. A guardian is a person who will look after the physical well-being of a child. A conservator is a person who will manage a child's assets and make payments from those assets for the child's benefit. Select them carefully. Also, before you select them, ask them whether they are willing and able to serve.

3.1   PERSONAL REPRESENTATIVE. (Name at least one)

I nominate _____ my wife, Holley Dodge Ford _____
(Insert name of person or eligible financial institution)

of _____ 8290 Lake Shore Drive, Grosse Point Farms, MI _____
(Insert address)
to serve as personal representative.

If my first choice does not serve, I nominate
_____ my son, Joe Louis Ford _____
(Insert name of person or eligible financial institution)

of _____ 29642 Lone Pine Road, Orchard Lake, MI _____
(Insert address)
to serve as personal representative.

Page 3 of _7_ pages

3.2 GUARDIAN AND CONSERVATOR.

Your spouse may die before you. Therefore, if you have a child under age 18, name an individual as guardian of the child, and an individual or eligible financial institution as conservator of the child's assets. The guardian and the conservator may, but need not be, the same person.

If a guardian or conservator is needed for any child of mine, I nominate

_____Allen Park, Jr._____
(Insert name of individual)

of _____423 Orchard Lake Rd., Kego Harbor, MI_____ as guardian
(Insert address)

and _____Allen Park, Jr._____
(Insert name of individual or eligible financial institution)

of _____423 Orchard Lake Rd., Kego Harbor, MI_____ as conservator.
(Insert address)

If my first choice cannot serve, I nominate

_____my daughter, Ann Allen Ford Fischer_____
(Insert name of individual)

of _____1637 E. River Road, Grosse Ile, MI_____ as guardian
(Insert address)

and _____National Bank of Detroit_____
(Insert name of individual or eligible financial institution)

of _____201 Jefferson Ave., Detroit, MI_____ as conservator.
(Insert address)

3.3 BOND.

A bond is a form of insurance in case your personal representative or a conservator performs improperly and jeopardizes your assets. A bond is not required. You may choose whether you wish to require your personal representative and any conservator to serve with or without bond. Bond premiums would be paid out of your assets.

(Select only one)

(a) My personal representative and any conservator I have named shall serve with bond.

_____
(Your Signature)

(b) My personal representative and any conservator I have named shall serve without bond.

_____*Henry Edsel Ford*_____
(Your Signature)

3.4 DEFINITIONS AND ADDITIONAL CLAUSES.

Definitions and additional clauses found at the end of this form are part of this will.

I sign my name to this Michigan statutory will on _____ October 23 _____, 20 _01_ .

Henry Edsel Ford

(Your Signature)

NOTICE REGARDING WITNESSES

You must use 2 adult witnesses who will not receive assets under this will as witnesses. It is preferable to have 3 adult witnesses. All the witnesses must observe you sign the will, have you tell them you signed the will, or have you tell them the will was signed at your direction in your presence.

STATEMENT OF WITNESSES

We sign below as witnesses, declaring that the individual who is making this will appears to be of sound mind and appears to be making this will freely, without duress, fraud, or undue influence, and that the individual making this will acknowledges that he or she has read, or has had it read to him or her, and understands the contents of this will.

Tom A. Edison

_____
(Print Name)
837 Pontiac Trail
_____
(Address)
Ann Arbor,   MI   48108
_____
(City)   (State)   (Zip)

Tom A. Edison
_____
(Signature of Witness)

Harvey Firestone IV
_____
(Print Name)
29305 Jolly Rd.
_____
(Address)
E. Lansing,   MI   48823
_____
(City)   (State)   (Zip)

Harvey Firestone IV
_____
(Signature of Witness)

John Johnson
_____
(Print Name)
25 Miner Street
_____
(Address)
Saugatuck,   MI   48623
_____
(City)   (State)   (Zip)

John Johnson
_____
(Signature of Witness)

Last Will and Testament

I, <u>John Smith</u> a resident of <u>Oakland</u> County, Michigan, declare this to be my will, hereby revoking any prior wills and codicils.

FIRST: I direct that all my debts and funeral expenses be paid out of my estate as soon after my death as is practicable.

SECOND: I may leave a separate statement or list disposing of certain items of my tangible personal property. Any such statement or list in existence at the time of my death shall be determinative with respect to all items bequeathed therein.

THIRD: I give, devise, and bequeath all my estate, real, personal, and mixed, of whatever kind and wherever situated, of which I may die seized or possessed, or in which I may have any interest or over which I may have any power of appointment or testamentary disposition, to my spouse, <u>Barbara Smith</u>. If my said spouse does not survive me, I give, and bequeath the said property to <u>my sisters, Jan Smith, Joan Smith, and Jennifer Smith Lee</u>, or the survivor of them.

FOURTH: In the event that any beneficiary fails to survive me by thirty days, then this will shall take effect as if that person had predeceased me.

FIFTH: I hereby nominate, constitute, and appoint <u>Barbara Smith</u> as Personal Representative of this, my Last Will and Testament. In the event that such named person is unable or unwilling to serve at any time or for any reason, then I nominate, constitute, and appoint <u>Reginald Smith</u> as Personal Representative in the place and stead of the person first named herein. It is my will and I direct that my Personal Representative shall not be required to furnish a bond for the faithful performance of his or her duties in any jurisdiction, any provision of law to the contrary notwithstanding, and I give my Personal Representative full power to administer my estate, including the power to settle claims, pay debts, and sell, lease or exchange real and personal property without court order.

IN WITNESS WHEREOF I have signed and published this Last Will and Testament, consisting of <u>2</u> page(s), this <u>23rd</u> day of <u>October</u>, <u>2001</u>.

John Smith
_____

STATEMENT OF WITNESSES

We sign below as witnesses, declaring that the person who is making this will appears to be of sound mind and appears to be making this will freely and without duress, fraud, or undue influence and that the person making this will acknowledges that he or she has read, or has had it read to them, and understands the contents of this will.

C. U. Sine	**Justin Cayce**
(Signature of Witness)	(Signature of Witness)
C.U. Sine	Justin Cayce
(Print Name)	(Print Name)
1428 N. Woodward Ave.	243 Maple Rd.
(Address)	(Address)
Royal Oak, MI 48073	Birmingham, MI 48009
(City) (State) (Zip)	(City) (State) (Zip)

Last Will and Testament
of

John Smith

I, _____ John Smith _____ a resident of _____ Kalamazoo _____ County, Michigan, declare this to be my will, hereby revoking any prior wills and codicils.

FIRST: I direct that all my debts and funeral expenses be paid out of my estate as soon after my death as is practicable.

SECOND: I may leave a separate statement or list disposing of certain items of my tangible personal property. Any such statement or list in existence at the time of my death shall be determinative with respect to all items bequeathed therein.

THIRD: I give, devise, and bequeath all my estate, real, personal, and mixed, of whatever kind and wherever situated, of which I may die seized or possessed, or in which I may have any interest or over which I may have any power of appointment or testamentary disposition, to my spouse, Barbara Smith _____. If my said spouse does not survive me, I give, and bequeath the said property to my children Amy Smith, Beamy Smith, and, Seamy Smith--, in equal shares or to their lineal descendants, per stirpes.

FOURTH: In the event that any beneficiary fails to survive me by thirty days, then this will shall take effect as if that person had predeceased me.

FIFTH: I hereby nominate, constitute, and appoint _____ Barbara Smith _____ as Personal Representative of this, my Last Will and Testament. In the event that such named person is unable or unwilling to serve at any time or for any reason, then I nominate, constitute, and appoint my brother, Reginald Smith as Personal Representative in the place and stead of the person first named herein. It is my will and I direct that my Personal Representative shall not be required to furnish a bond for the faithful performance of his or her duties in any jurisdiction, any provision of law to the contrary notwithstanding, and I give my Personal Representative full power to administer my estate, including the power to settle claims, pay debts, and sell, lease or exchange real and personal property without court order.

Testator Initials: _____

IN WITNESS WHEREOF I have signed and published this Last Will and Testament, consisting of two pages, this ___5th___ day of ___January___, ___2002___.

John Smith
_____

STATEMENT OF WITNESSES

We sign below as witnesses, declaring that the person who is making this will appears to be of sound mind and appears to be making this will freely and without duress, fraud, or undue influence and that the person making this will acknowledges that he or she has read, or has had it read to them, and understands the contents of this will.

C.U. Sine
_____
(Print Name)

C. U. Sine
_____
(Signature of Witness)

1428 N. Woodward Ave.
_____
(Address)

Royal Oak,   MI   48073
_____
(City)   (State)   (Zip)

Justin Cayce
_____
(Print Name)

Justin Cayce
_____
(Signature of Witness)

243 Maple Rd.
_____
(Address)

Birmingham,   MI   48009
_____
(City)   (State)   (Zip)

Page 2 of 3 pages

Last Will and Testament
of

<u>John Doe</u>

I, _____<u>John Doe</u>_____ a resident of _____<u>Kent</u>_____ County, Michigan, declare this to be my will, hereby revoking any prior wills and codicils.

FIRST: I direct that all my debts and funeral expenses be paid out of my estate as soon after my death as is practicable.

SECOND: I may leave a separate statement or list disposing of certain items of my tangible personal property. Any such statement or list in existence at the time of my death shall be determinative with respect to all items bequeathed therein.

THIRD: I give, devise, and bequeath all my estate, real, personal, and mixed, of whatever kind and wherever situated, of which I may die seized or possessed, or in which I may have any interest or over which I may have any power of appointment or testamentary disposition, to my children _____<u>James Doe, Mary Doe, Larry Doe, Barry Doe, Carrie Doe, and Moe Doe</u>_____ plus any afterborn or adopted children in equal shares or to their lineal descendants per stirpes.

FOURTH: In the event that any beneficiary fails to survive me by thirty days, then this will shall take effect as if that person had predeceased me.

FIFTH: In the event any of my children have not attained the age of 18 years at the time of my death, I hereby nominate, constitute, and appoint <u>my brother, Herbert Doe</u> as guardian over the person of any of my children who have not reached the age of majority at the time of my death. In the event that said guardian is unable or unwilling to serve, then I nominate, constitute, and appoint <u>my brother Tom Doe</u> as guardian. Said guardian shall serve without bond or surety.

SIXTH: In the event any of my children have not attained the age of 18 years at the time of my death, I hereby nominate, constitute, and appoint <u>my brother Clarence Doe</u> as conservator over the property of any of my children who have not reached the age of majority at the time of my death. In the event that said conservator is unable or unwilling to serve, then I nominate, constitute, and appoint <u>my brother Englebert Doe</u> as conservator. Said conservator shall serve without bond or surety.

Testator Initials: _____

Page 1 of 3 pages

SEVENTH: I hereby nominate, constitute, and appoint <u>my brother, Clarence Doe</u> as Personal Representative of this, my Last Will and Testament. In the event that such named person is unable or unwilling to serve at any time or for any reason, then I nominate, constitute, and appoint <u>my brother, Englebert Doe</u> as Personal Representative in the place and stead of the person first named herein. It is my will and I direct that my Personal Representative shall not be required to furnish a bond for the faithful performance of his or her duties in any jurisdiction, any provision of law to the contrary notwithstanding, and I give my Personal Representative full power to administer my estate, including the power to settle claims, pay debts, and sell, lease or exchange real and personal property without court order.

IN WITNESS WHEREOF I have signed and published this Last Will and Testament, consisting of two pages, this <u>2nd</u> day of <u>July</u>, <u>2001</u>.

John Doe _____

STATEMENT OF WITNESSES

We sign below as witnesses, declaring that the person who is making this will appears to be of sound mind and appears to be making this will freely and without duress, fraud, or undue influence and that the person making this will acknowledges that he or she has read, or has had it read to them, and understands the contents of this will.

<u>C.U. Sine</u>
      (Print Name)
<u>5628 Alpine Ave.</u>
      (Address)
<u>Grand Rapids, MI</u>   <u>49512</u>
(City)   (State)   (Zip)

C. U. Sine _____
    (Signature of Witness)

<u>Justin Cayce</u>
      (Print Name)
<u>94 Grandville Ave.</u>
      (Address)
<u>Grand Rapids, MI</u>   <u>49546</u>
(City)   (State)   (Zip)

Justin Cayce _____
    (Signature of Witness)

Page 2 of <u>3</u> pages

STATE OF MICHIGAN

COUNTY OF _____Kent_____

I, _____John Doe_____, the testator, sign my name to this document on _May 27_ ,2001_. I have taken an oath, administered by the officer whose signature and seal appear on this document, swearing that the statements in this document are true. I declare to that officer that this document is my will; that I sign it willingly or willingly direct another to sign for me; that I execute it as my voluntary act for the purposes expressed in this will; and that I am 18 years of age or older, of sound mind, and under no constraint or undue influence.

_____
John Doe
(Signature) Testator

We, _C.U. Sine_____ and _Justin Cayce_____, the witnesses, sign our names to this document and have taken an oath, administered by the officer whose signature and seal appear on this document, to swear that all of the following statements are true: the individual signing this document as the testator executes the document as his or her will, signs it willingly or willingly directs another to sign for him or her, and executes it as his or her voluntary act for the purposes expressed in this will; each of us, in the testator's presence, signs this will as witness to the testator's signing; and, to the best of our knowledge, the testator is 18 years of age or older, of sound mind, and under no constraint or undue influence.

_____
Justin Cayce
Signature (Witness)

C.U. Sine
_____
(Signature) Witness

The State of _Michigan_____
County of _Kent_____

Sworn to and signed in my presence by _John Doe_, the testator, and sworn to and signed in my presence by _C.U. Sine____ and _Justin Cayce____, witnesses, on_____May   27_____, _2001_____ .month/day/year

_____
(SEAL) Signed
Notary Public
My Commission Expires:

Page _3_ of _3_ pages

Codicil to the Will of

_____Stirling Heitz_____

I, _____Stirling Heitz_____, a resident of _____Macomb_____ County, Michigan, declare this to be the first codicil to my Last Will and Testament dated _____January 5_____, _____1993_____.

FIRST: I hereby revoke the clause of my Will which reads as follows: _____
FOURTH: I hereby leave $5,000.00 to my daughter Mildred. _____

_____

_____.

SECOND: I hereby add the following clause to my Will: _____
FOURTH: I hereby leave $1,000.00 to my daughter Mildred. _____

_____

_____.

THIRD: In all other respects I hereby confirm and republish my Last Will and Testament dated _____January 5_____, _____1993_____.

IN WITNESS WHEREOF, I have signed and published the foregoing instrument as and for a codicil to my Last Will and Testament, this _23rd_ day of _____August_____, _2001_

_____***Stirling Heitz***_____

STATEMENT OF WITNESSES

We sign below as witnesses, declaring that the person who is making this will appears to be of sound mind and appears to be making this will freely and without duress, fraud, or undue influence and that the person making this will acknowledges that he or she has read, or has had it read to them, and understands the contents of this will.

Hazel Parke	**Bob Lowe**
(Signature of Witness)	(Signature of Witness)
Hazel Parke	Bob Lowe
(Print Name)	(Print Name)
192 Oakwood Blvd.	819 Eureka Ave.
(Address)	(Address)
Dearborn, MI 48124	Southgate, MI 48195
(City)　(State)　(Zip)	(City)　(State)　(Zip)

Designation of Patient Advocate and Living Will

I, _____Tiny Tim Cratchet_____, appoint _____Bob Cratchet_____, whose address is _217 Christmas Past Circle, Bloomfield Hills, MI_ and whose telephone number is _(810) 555-5555_, as my patient advocate pursuant to M.S.A. §27.5496; M.C.L.A. §700.496. I appoint _____Mary Cratchet_____, whose address is _217 Christmas Past Circle, Bloomfield Hills, MI_ and whose telephone number is _(810) 555-5555_, as my alternate patient advocate in the event my patient advocate designated above does not accept the appointment, is incapacitated, or is removed. I authorize my patient advocate to make health care decisions for me when I am incapable of making my own heath care decisions, including decisions to withhold or withdraw medical treatment, even if such withholding or withdrawal could or would allow me to die. I understand the consequences of appointing a patient advocate.

I direct that my agent comply with the following instructions or limitations:
_____none_____
_____.

I also direct that my patient advocate have authority to make decisions regarding the enforcement of my intentions regarding life-prolonging procedures as stated below:

I, _____Tiny Tim Cratchet_____, being of sound mind willfully and voluntarily make known my desire that my dying shall not be artificially prolonged under the circumstances set forth below, do hereby declare:

If I should have an incurable or irreversible condition that will cause my death within a relatively short time, and if I am unable to make decisions regarding my medical treatment, I direct my attending physician to withhold or withdraw procedures that merely prolong the dying process and are not necessary to my comfort, or to alleviate pain.

This authorization [check only one box] ❑ includes ☒ does not include the withholding or withdrawal of artificial feeding and hydration.

Signed this _23rd_ day of _____June_____, _2001_.

Tiny Tim Cratchet
_____
Signature
Address: _217 Christmas Past Circle_
Bloomfield Hills, MI 48302

The declarant is personally known to me and voluntarily signed this document in my presence.

Witness: *Ebenezer Scrooge* | Witness: *Charles Dickens*
Name: _Ebenezer Scrooge_ | Name: _Charles Dickens_
Address: _14285 Marley Ghost Dr._ | Address: _452 Copperfield Ln._
Auburn Hills, MI 48321 | _Saugatuck, MI 49453_

Acceptance of Patient Advocate

I HEREBY accept the appointment as patient advocate and understand that:

(a)   This designation shall not become effective unless the patient is unable to participate in medical decisions.

(b)   A patient advocate shall not exercise powers concerning the patient's care, custody, and medical treatment that the patient, if the patient were able to participate in the decision, could not have exercised on his or her own behalf.

(c)   This designation cannot be used to make a medical treatment decision to withhold or withdraw treatment from a patient who is pregnant that would result in the pregnant patient's death.

(d)   A patient advocate may make a decision to withhold or withdraw treatment which would allow a patient to die only if the patient has expressed in a clear and convincing manner that the patient advocate is authorized to make such a decision, and that the patient acknowledges that such a decision could or would allow the patient's death.

(e)   A patient advocate shall not receive compensation for the performance of his or her authority, rights, and responsibilities, but a patient advocate may be reimbursed for actual and necessary expenses incurred in the performance of his or her authority, rights, and responsibilities.

(f)   A patient advocate shall act in accordance with the standards of care applicable to fiduciaries when acting for the patient and shall act consistent with the patient's best interests. The known desires of the patient expressed or evidenced while the patient is able to participate in medical treatment decisions are presumed to be in the patient's best interests.

(g)   A patient may revoke his or her designation at any time and in any manner sufficient to communicate an intent to revoke.

(h)   A patient advocate may revoke his or her acceptance to the designation at any time and in any manner sufficient to communicate an intent to revoke.

(i)   A patient admitted to a health facility or agency has the rights enumerated in section 20201 of the public health code, Act No. 368 of the Public Acts of 1978, being section 33.20201 of the Michigan Compiled Laws.

Date: __June 23, 2001__

Bob Cratchet
Signature

APPENDIX C
BLANK FORMS

The following pages contain forms that can be used to prepare a will, codicil, designation of patient advocate and living will, and uniform donor card. They should only be used by persons who have read this book, who do not have any complications in their legal affairs, and who understand the forms they are using. The forms may be used right out of the book or they may be photocopied or retyped. It may be a good idea to use photocopies so you will have the originals in the book in case you make a mistake.

How to Pick the Right Will

If you do not use the MICHIGAN STATUTORY FORM (form 3), you can follow this chart to find the right will for your situation. Then use form 18 for the SELF-PROVING WILL AFFIDAVIT.

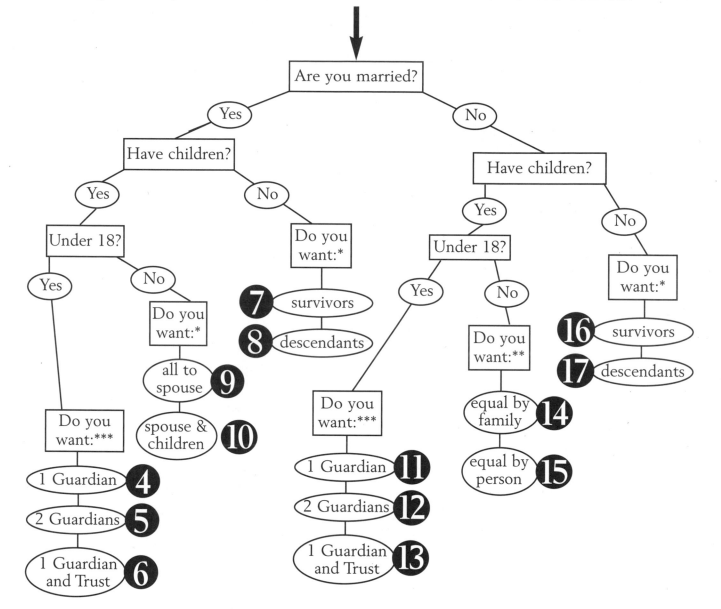

18 Use the SELF-PROVING WILL AFFIDAVIT with all wills

* For an explanation of survivors/descendants, see pages 27-29.
** For an explanation of families/persons, see pages 27-29.
*** For an explanation of children's guardians and trust, see pages 30-31.

Asset and Beneficiary List

Property Inventory

Assets

Bank Accounts (checking, savings, certificates of deposit)

_____

_____

_____

_____

_____

_____

_____

Real Estate

_____

_____

_____

_____

_____

_____

_____

Vehicles (cars, trucks, boats, planes, RVs, etc.)

_____

_____

_____

_____

_____

_____

_____

Personal Property (collections, jewelry, tools, artwork, household items, etc.)

_____

_____

_____

_____

_____

_____

_____

_____

_____

_____

_____

_____

_____

_____

Stocks/Bonds/Mutual Funds

_____

_____

_____

_____

_____

_____

_____

_____

_____

_____

_____

Retirement Accounts (IRAs, 401(k)s, pension plans, etc.)

_____

_____

_____

_____

_____

_____

Receivables (mortgages held, notes, accounts receivable, personal loans)

_____

_____

_____

_____

Life Insurance

_____

_____

_____

_____

_____

_____

Other Property (trusts, partnerships, businesses, profit sharing, copyrights, etc.)

_____

_____

_____

_____

_____

_____

Liabilities

Real Estate Loans

_____

_____

_____

_____

_____

_____

Vehicle Loans

_____

_____

_____

_____

_____

_____

_____

Other Secured Loans

_____

_____

_____

_____

_____

_____

_____

Unsecured Loans and Debts (taxes, child support, judgments, etc.)

_____

_____

_____

_____

_____

_____

_____

Beneficiary List

Name_____ Address_____ Phone_____
_____

Name_____ Address_____ Phone_____
_____

Name_____ Address_____ Phone_____
_____

Name_____ Address_____ Phone_____
_____

Name_____ Address_____ Phone_____
_____

Preferences and Information List

STATEMENT OF DESIRES AND LOCATION OF PROPERTY & DOCUMENTS

I, _____, am signing this document as the expression of my desires as to the matters stated below, and to inform my family members or other significant persons of the location of certain property and documents in the event of any emergency or of my death.

1.   **Funeral Desires.** It is my desire that the following arrangements be made for my funeral and disposition of remains in the event of my death (state if you have made any arrangements, such as pre-paid burial plans, cemetery plots owned, etc.):

❑   Burial at _____

❑   Cremation at _____

❑   Other specific desires: _____

2.   **Pets.** I have the following pet(s): _____

_____. The following are my desires concerning the care of said pet(s): _____

4.   **Notification.** I would like the following person(s) notified in the event of emergency or death (give name, address and phone number):

_____

_____

_____

5.   **Location of Documents.** The following is a list of important documents, and their location:

❑   Last Will and Testament, dated _____. Location: _____

❑   Durable Power of Attorney, dated _____. Location: _____

❑   Living Will, dated _____. Location: _____

❑   Deed(s) to real estate (describe property location and location of deed):

_____

_____

❏   Title(s) to vehicles (cars, boats, etc.) (Describe vehicle, its location, and location of title, registration, or other documents):

_____
_____
_____
_____

❏   Life insurance policies (list name address & phone number of insurance company and insurance agent, policy number, and location of policy):

_____
_____
_____

❏   Other insurance policies (list type, company & agent, policy number, and location of policy):

_____
_____
_____

❏   Other: (list other documents such as stock certificates, bonds, certificates of deposit, etc., and their location):

_____
_____
_____

6.   **Location of Assets.** In addition to items readily visible in my home or listed above, I have the following assets:

❏   Safe deposit box located at _____
     Box number _____ Key located at: _____

❏   Bank accounts (list name & address of bank, type of account, and account number):

_____
_____
_____
_____

❏   Other (describe the item and give its location):

_____
_____
_____
_____

7.   Other desires or information (state any desires or provide any information not given above; use additional sheets of paper if necessary):

_____
_____
_____
_____
_____

Dated: _____   _____
                                    Signature

MICHIGAN STATUTORY WILL
NOTICE

1. An individual age 18 or older and of sound mind may sign a will.
2. There are several kinds of wills. If you choose to complete this form, you will have a Michigan statutory will. If this will does not meet your wishes in any way, you should talk with a lawyer before choosing a Michigan statutory will.
3. Warning! It is strongly recommended that you do not add or cross out any words on this form except for filling in the blanks because all or part of this will may not be valid if you do so.
4. This will has no effect on jointly held assets, on retirement plan benefits, or on life insurance on your life if you have named a beneficiary who survives you.
5. This will is not designed to reduce estate taxes.
6. This will treats adopted children and children born outside of wedlock who would inherit if their parent died without a will the same way as children born or conceived during marriage.
7. You should keep this will in your safe deposit box or other safe place. By paying a small fee, you may file this will in your county's probate court for safekeeping. You should tell your family where the will is kept.
8. You may make and sign a new will at any time. If you marry or divorce after you sign this will, you should make and sign a new will.

INSTRUCTIONS:

1. To have a Michigan statutory will, you must complete the blanks on the will form. You may do this yourself, or direct someone to do it for you. You must either sign the will or direct someone else to sign it in your name and in your presence.
2. Read the entire Michigan statutory will carefully before you begin filling in the blanks. If there is anything you do not understand, you should ask a lawyer to explain it to you.

MICHIGAN STATUTORY WILL OF

_____

(Print or type your full name)

ARTICLE 1. DECLARATIONS

This is my will and I revoke any prior wills and codicils. I live in _____ County, Michigan.

My spouse is _____
(Insert spouse's name or write "None")

My children now living are:

_____   _____

(Insert names or write "None")

_____   _____

_____   _____

Page 1 of ___ pages

ARTICLE 2. DISPOSITION OF MY ASSETS

2.1 CASH GIFTS TO PERSONS OR CHARITIES. (Optional)

I can leave no more that two (2) cash gifts. I make the following cash gifts to the persons or charities in the amounts stated here. Any transfer tax due upon my death shall be paid from the balance of my estate and not from these gifts.

Full name and address of person or charity to receive cash gift.
(Name only one (1) person or charity here)

_____
(Insert name of person or charity)

_____
(Insert address)

AMOUNT OF GIFT (In figures): $_____

AMOUNT OF GIFT (In words): $_____ Dollars

_____
(Your Signature)

Full name and address of person or charity to receive cash gift.
(Name only one (1) person or charity here)

_____
(Insert name of person or charity)

_____
(Insert address)

AMOUNT OF GIFT (In figures): $_____

AMOUNT OF GIFT (In words): $_____ Dollars

_____
(Your Signature)

2.2 PERSONAL AND HOUSEHOLD ITEMS.

I may leave a separate list or statement either in my handwriting or signed by me at the end, regarding gifts of specific books, jewelry, clothing, automobiles, furniture, and other personal and household items.

I give my spouse all my books, jewelry, clothing, automobiles, furniture, and other personal and household items not included on any such separate list or statement. If I am not married at the time I sign this will, or if my spouse dies before me, my personal representative shall distribute those items, as equally as possible, among my children who survive me. If no children survive me, these items shall be distributed as set forth in paragraph 2.3.

2.3 ALL OTHER ASSETS.

I give everything else I own to my spouse. If I am not married at the time I sign this will, or if my spouse dies before me, I give these assets to my children and the descendants of any deceased child. If no spouse, children, or descendants of children survive me, I choose one of the following distribution clauses by signing my name on the line after that clause. If I sign on both lines, or if I fail to sign on either line, or if I am not now married, these assets will go under distribution clause (b).

Distribution clause, if no spouse, children, or descendants of children survive me (Select only one).
(a)   One-half to be distributed to my heirs as if I did not have a will, and one-half to be distributed to my spouse's heirs as if my spouse had died just after me without a will.

_____
(Your Signature)

(b)   All to be distributed to my heirs as if I did not have a will.

_____
(Your Signature)

ARTICLE 3. NOMINATIONS OF PERSONAL REPRESENTATIVE, GUARDIAN, AND CONSERVATOR

Personal representatives, guardians, and conservators have a great deal of responsibility. The role of a personal representative is to collect your assets, pay debts and taxes from those assets, and distribute the remaining assets as directed in the will. A guardian is a person who will look after the physical well-being of a child. A conservator is a person who will manage a child's assets and make payments from those assets for the child's benefit. Select them carefully. Also, before you select them, ask them whether they are willing and able to serve.

3.1   PERSONAL REPRESENTATIVE. (Name at least one)

I nominate _____
(Insert name of person or eligible financial institution)

of _____
(Insert address)
to serve as personal representative.

If my first choice does not serve, I nominate

_____
(Insert name of person or eligible financial institution)

of _____
(Insert address)
to serve as personal representative.

Page 3 of ___ pages

3.2   GUARDIAN AND CONSERVATOR.

Your spouse may die before you. Therefore, if you have a child under age 18, name an individual as guardian of the child, and an individual or eligible financial institution as conservator of the child's assets. The guardian and the conservator may, but need not be, the same person.

If a guardian or conservator is needed for any child of mine, I nominate

_____
(Insert name of individual)

of _____ as guardian
(Insert address)

and _____
(Insert name of individual or eligible financial institution)

of _____ as conservator.
(Insert address)

If my first choice cannot serve, I nominate

_____
(Insert name of individual)

of _____ as guardian
(Insert address)

and _____
(Insert name of individual or eligible financial institution)

of _____ as conservator.
(Insert address)

3.3   BOND.

A bond is a form of insurance in case your personal representative or a conservator performs improperly and jeopardizes your assets. A bond is not required. You may choose whether you wish to require your personal representative and any conservator to serve with or without bond. Bond premiums would be paid out of your assets.

(Select only one)

(a) My personal representative and any conservator I have named shall serve with bond.

_____
(Your Signature)

(b) My personal representative and any conservator I have named shall serve without bond.

_____
(Your Signature)

3.4 DEFINITIONS AND ADDITIONAL CLAUSES.

Definitions and additional clauses found at the end of this form are part of this will.

I sign my name to this Michigan statutory will on _____, 20_____.

_____
(Your Signature)

NOTICE REGARDING WITNESSES

You must use 2 adult witnesses who will not receive assets under this will as witnesses. It is preferable to have 3 adult witnesses. All the witnesses must observe you sign the will, have you tell them you signed the will, or have you tell them the will was signed at your direction in your presence.

STATEMENT OF WITNESSES

We sign below as witnesses, declaring that the individual who is making this will appears to be of sound mind and appears to be making this will freely, without duress, fraud, or undue influence, and that the individual making this will acknowledges that he or she has read, or has had it read to him or her, and understands the contents of this will.

_____   _____
(Print Name)   (Signature of Witness)

_____
(Address)

_____
(City)   (State)   (Zip)

_____   _____
(Print Name)   (Signature of Witness)

_____
(Address)

_____
(City)   (State)   (Zip)

_____   _____
(Print Name)   (Signature of Witness)

_____
(Address)

_____
(City)   (State)   (Zip)

This page intentionally left blank.

Last Will and Testament
of

_____

I, _____ a resident of _____
County, Michigan, declare this to be my will, hereby revoking any prior wills and codicils.

FIRST: I direct that all my debts and funeral expenses be paid out of my estate as soon
after my death as is practicable.

SECOND: I may leave a separate statement or list disposing of certain items of my
tangible personal property. Any such statement or list in existence at the time of my death
shall be determinative with respect to all items bequeathed therein.

THIRD: I give, devise, and bequeath all my estate, real, personal, and mixed, of whatever kind and wherever situated, of which I may die seized or possessed, or in which I may
have any interest or over which I may have any power of appointment or testamentary disposition, to my spouse, _____. If my said spouse does not
survive me, I give, and bequeath the said property to my children _____
_____
_____,
plus any afterborn or adopted children in equal shares or their lineal descendants, per stirpes.

FOURTH: In the event that any beneficiary fails to survive me by thirty days, then
this will shall take effect as if that person had predeceased me.

FIFTH: Should my spouse not survive me, I hereby nominate, constitute, and appoint
_____ as guardian over the person and as conser-
vator over the estate of any of my children who have not reached the age of majority at the
time of my death. In the event that said guardian/conservator is unable or unwilling to serve,
then I nominate, constitute, and appoint _____ as
guardian/conservator. Said guardian shall serve without bond or surety.

SIXTH: I hereby nominate, constitute, and appoint _____
as Personal Representative of this, my Last Will and Testament. In the event that such named
person is unable or unwilling to serve at any time or for any reason, then I nominate, constitute, and appoint _____ as Personal Representative in the
place and stead of the person first named herein. It is my will and I direct that my Personal
Representative shall not be required to furnish a bond for the faithful performance of his or

Testator Initials: _____

Page 1 of ___ pages

her duties in any jurisdiction, any provision of law to the contrary notwithstanding, and I give my Personal Representative full power to administer my estate, including the power to settle claims, pay debts, and sell, lease or exchange real and personal property without court order.

IN WITNESS WHEREOF I have signed and published this Last Will and Testament, consisting of two pages, this _____ day of _____, _____.

_____

STATEMENT OF WITNESSES

We sign below as witnesses, declaring that the person who is making this will appears to be of sound mind and appears to be making this will freely and without duress, fraud, or undue influence and that the person making this will acknowledges that he or she has read, or has had it read to them, and understands the contents of this will.

| _____ | _____ |
| (Print Name) | (Signature of Witness) |

_____
(Address)

_____
(City)   (State)   (Zip)

| _____ | _____ |
| (Print Name) | (Signature of Witness) |

_____
(Address)

_____
(City)   (State)   (Zip)

Page 2 of ___ pages

Last Will and Testament
of

_____

I, _____ a resident of _____ County, Michigan, declare this to be my will, hereby revoking any prior wills and codicils.

FIRST: I direct that all my debts and funeral expenses be paid out of my estate as soon after my death as is practicable.

SECOND: I may leave a separate statement or list disposing of certain items of my tangible personal property. Any such statement or list in existence at the time of my death shall be determinative with respect to all items bequeathed therein.

THIRD: I give, devise, and bequeath all my estate, real, personal, and mixed, of whatever kind and wherever situated, of which I may die seized or possessed, or in which I may have any interest or over which I may have any power of appointment or testamentary disposition, to my spouse, _____. If my said spouse does not survive me, I give, and bequeath the said property to my children _____

_____

_____, plus any afterborn or adopted children in equal shares or their lineal descendants, per stirpes.

FOURTH: In the event that any beneficiary fails to survive me by thirty days, then this will shall take effect as if that person had predeceased me.

FIFTH: Should my spouse not survive me, I hereby nominate, constitute, and appoint _____, as guardian over the person of any of my children who have not reached the age of majority at the time of my death. In the event that said guardian is unable or unwilling to serve, then I nominate, constitute, and appoint _____ as guardian. Said guardian shall serve without bond or surety.

SIXTH: Should my spouse not survive me, I hereby nominate, constitute, and appoint _____ as conservator over the estate of any of my children who have not reached the age of majority at the time of my death. In the event that said conservator is unable or unwilling to serve, then I nominate, constitute, and appoint _____ as conservator. Said conservator shall serve without bond or surety.

Testator Initials: _____

SEVENTH: I hereby nominate, constitute, and appoint _____ as Personal Representative of this, my Last Will and Testament. In the event that such named person is unable or unwilling to serve at any time or for any reason, then I nominate, constitute, and appoint _____ as Personal Representative in the place and stead of the person first named herein. It is my will and I direct that my Personal Representative shall not be required to furnish a bond for the faithful performance of his or her duties in any jurisdiction, any provision of law to the contrary notwithstanding, and I give my Personal Representative full power to administer my estate, including the power to settle claims, pay debts, and sell, lease or exchange real and personal property without court order.

IN WITNESS WHEREOF I have signed and published this Last Will and Testament, consisting of two pages, this _____ day of _____, _____.

_____

STATEMENT OF WITNESSES

We sign below as witnesses, declaring that the person who is making this will appears to be of sound mind and appears to be making this will freely and without duress, fraud, or undue influence and that the person making this will acknowledges that he or she has read, or has had it read to them, and understands the contents of this will.

_____	_____
(Print Name)	(Signature of Witness)
_____	
(Address)	
_____	
(City) (State) (Zip)	

_____	_____
(Print Name)	(Signature of Witness)
_____	
(Address)	
_____	
(City) (State) (Zip)	

Last Will and Testament
of

_____

I, _____ a resident of _____ County, Michigan, declare this to be my will, hereby revoking any prior wills and codicils.

FIRST: I direct that all my debts and funeral expenses be paid out of my estate as soon after my death as is practicable.

SECOND: I may leave a separate statement or list disposing of certain items of my tangible personal property. Any such statement or list in existence at the time of my death shall be determinative with respect to all items bequeathed therein.

THIRD: I give, devise, and bequeath all my estate, real, personal, and mixed, of whatever kind and wherever situated, of which I may die seized or possessed, or in which I may have any interest or over which I may have any power of appointment or testamentary disposition, to my spouse, _____. If my said spouse does not survive me, I give, and bequeath the said property to my children _____
_____
_____,
plus any afterborn or adopted children in equal shares or their lineal descendants, per stirpes.

FOURTH: In the event that any beneficiary fails to survive me by thirty days, then this will shall take effect as if that person had predeceased me.

FIFTH: In the event that any of my children have not reached the age of _____ years at the time of my death, then the share of any such child shall be held in a separate trust by _____ for such child.

The trustee shall use the income and that part of the principal of the trust as is, in the trustee's sole discretion, necessary or desirable to provide proper housing, medical care, food, clothing, entertainment and education for the trust beneficiary, considering the beneficiary's other resources. Any income that is not distributed shall be added to the principal. Additionally, the trustee shall have all powers conferred by the law of the state having jurisdiction over this trust, as well as the power to pay from the assets of the trust reasonable fees necessary to administer the trust.

The trust shall terminate when the child reaches the age specified above and the remaining assets distributed to the child, unless they have been exhausted sooner. In the event the child dies prior to the termination of the trust, then the assets shall pass to the estate of the child. The interests of the beneficiary under this trust shall not be assignable and shall be free from the claims of creditors to the full extent allowed by law.

Testator Initials: _____

Page 1 of ___ pages

101

In the event the said trustee is unable or unwilling to serve for any reason, then I nominate, constitute, and appoint _____as alternate trustee. No bond shall be required of either trustee in any jurisdiction and this trust shall be administered without court supervision as allowed by law.

SIXTH: Should my spouse not survive me, I hereby nominate, constitute, and appoint _____as guardian over the person of any of my children who have not reached the age of majority at the time of my death. In the event that said guardian is unable or unwilling to serve, then I nominate, constitute, and appoint _____ _____ as guardian.

SEVENTH: I hereby nominate, constitute, and appoint _____ as Personal Representative of this, my Last Will and Testament. In the event that such named person is unable or unwilling to serve at any time or for any reason, then I nominate, constitute, and appoint _____ as Personal Representative in the place and stead of the person first named herein. It is my will and I direct that my Personal Representative shall not be required to furnish a bond for the faithful performance of his or her duties in any jurisdiction, any provision of law to the contrary notwithstanding, and I give my Personal Representative full power to administer my estate, including the power to settle claims, pay debts, and sell, lease or exchange real and personal property without court order.

IN WITNESS WHEREOF I have signed and published this Last Will and Testament, consisting of two pages, this _____ day of _____, _____.

_____

STATEMENT OF WITNESSES

We sign below as witnesses, declaring that the person who is making this will appears to be of sound mind and appears to be making this will freely and without duress, fraud, or undue influence and that the person making this will acknowledges that he or she has read, or has had it read to them, and understands the contents of this will.

_____	_____
(Signature of Witness)	(Signature of Witness)
_____	_____
(Print Name)	(Print Name)
_____	_____
(Address)	(Address)

| _____ | _____ | _____ | _____ | _____ | _____ |
| (City) | (State) | (Zip) | (City) | (State) | (Zip) |

Last Will and Testament

I, _____ a resident of _____ County, Michigan, declare this to be my will, hereby revoking any prior wills and codicils.

FIRST: I direct that all my debts and funeral expenses be paid out of my estate as soon after my death as is practicable.

SECOND: I may leave a separate statement or list disposing of certain items of my tangible personal property. Any such statement or list in existence at the time of my death shall be determinative with respect to all items bequeathed therein.

THIRD: I give, devise, and bequeath all my estate, real, personal, and mixed, of whatever kind and wherever situated, of which I may die seized or possessed, or in which I may have any interest or over which I may have any power of appointment or testamentary disposition, to my spouse, _____. If my said spouse does not survive me, I give, and bequeath the said property to _____ _____, or the survivor of them.

FOURTH: In the event that any beneficiary fails to survive me by thirty days, then this will shall take effect as if that person had predeceased me.

FIFTH: I hereby nominate, constitute, and appoint _____ as Personal Representative of this, my Last Will and Testament. In the event that such named person is unable or unwilling to serve at any time or for any reason, then I nominate, constitute, and appoint _____ as Personal Representative in the place and stead of the person first named herein. It is my will and I direct that my Personal Representative shall not be required to furnish a bond for the faithful performance of his or her duties in any jurisdiction, any provision of law to the contrary notwithstanding, and I give my Personal Representative full power to administer my estate, including the power to settle claims, pay debts, and sell, lease or exchange real and personal property without court order.

IN WITNESS WHEREOF I have signed and published this Last Will and Testament, consisting of two pages, this _____ day of _____, _____.

_____

STATEMENT OF WITNESSES

We sign below as witnesses, declaring that the person who is making this will appears to be of sound mind and appears to be making this will freely and without duress, fraud, or undue influence and that the person making this will acknowledges that he or she has read, or has had it read to them, and understands the contents of this will.

_____	_____
(Signature of Witness)	(Signature of Witness)
_____	_____
(Print Name)	(Print Name)
_____	_____
(Address)	(Address)
(City) (State) (Zip)	(City) (State) (Zip)

This page intentionally left blank.

Last Will and Testament
of

_____

I, _____ a resident of _____ County, Michigan, declare this to be my will, hereby revoking any prior wills and codicils.

FIRST: I direct that all my debts and funeral expenses be paid out of my estate as soon after my death as is practicable.

SECOND: I may leave a separate statement or list disposing of certain items of my tangible personal property. Any such statement or list in existence at the time of my death shall be determinative with respect to all items bequeathed therein.

THIRD: I give, devise, and bequeath all my estate, real, personal, and mixed, of whatever kind and wherever situated, of which I may die seized or possessed, or in which I may have any interest or over which I may have any power of appointment or testamentary disposition, to my spouse, _____. If my said spouse does not survive me, I give, and bequeath the said property to _____ _____ _____ _____, or to their lineal descendants, per stirpes.

FOURTH: In the event that any beneficiary fails to survive me by thirty days, then this will shall take effect as if that person had predeceased me.

FIFTH: I hereby nominate, constitute, and appoint _____ as Personal Representative of this, my Last Will and Testament. In the event that such named person is unable or unwilling to serve at any time or for any reason, then I nominate, constitute, and appoint _____ as Personal Representative in the place and stead of the person first named herein. It is my will and I direct that my Personal Representative shall not be required to furnish a bond for the faithful performance of his or her duties in any jurisdiction, any provision of law to the contrary notwithstanding, and I give my Personal Representative full power to administer my estate, including the power to settle claims, pay debts, and sell, lease or exchange real and personal property without court order.

Testator Initials: _____

Page 1 of ___ pages

105

IN WITNESS WHEREOF I have signed and published this Last Will and Testament, consisting of two pages, this _____ day of _____, _____.

_____

STATEMENT OF WITNESSES

We sign below as witnesses, declaring that the person who is making this will appears to be of sound mind and appears to be making this will freely and without duress, fraud, or undue influence and that the person making this will acknowledges that he or she has read, or has had it read to them, and understands the contents of this will.

_____   _____
(Print Name)   (Signature of Witness)

_____
(Address)

_____
(City)   (State)   (Zip)

_____   _____
(Print Name)   (Signature of Witness)

_____
(Address)

_____
(City)   (State)   (Zip)

Last Will and Testament
of

_____

I, _____ a resident of _____ County, Michigan, declare this to be my will, hereby revoking any prior wills and codicils.

FIRST: I direct that all my debts and funeral expenses be paid out of my estate as soon after my death as is practicable.

SECOND: I may leave a separate statement or list disposing of certain items of my tangible personal property. Any such statement or list in existence at the time of my death shall be determinative with respect to all items bequeathed therein.

THIRD: I give, devise, and bequeath all my estate, real, personal, and mixed, of whatever kind and wherever situated, of which I may die seized or possessed, or in which I may have any interest or over which I may have any power of appointment or testamentary disposition, to my spouse, _____. If my said spouse does not survive me, I give, and bequeath the said property to my children _____

_____

_____

_____,

in equal shares or to their lineal descendants, per stirpes.

FOURTH: In the event that any beneficiary fails to survive me by thirty days, then this will shall take effect as if that person had predeceased me.

FIFTH: I hereby nominate, constitute, and appoint _____ as Personal Representative of this, my Last Will and Testament. In the event that such named person is unable or unwilling to serve at any time or for any reason, then I nominate, constitute, and appoint _____ as Personal Representative in the place and stead of the person first named herein. It is my will and I direct that my Personal Representative shall not be required to furnish a bond for the faithful performance of his or her duties in any jurisdiction, any provision of law to the contrary notwithstanding, and I give my Personal Representative full power to administer my estate, including the power to settle claims, pay debts, and sell, lease or exchange real and personal property without court order.

Testator Initials: _____

Page 1 of ___ pages

IN WITNESS WHEREOF I have signed and published this Last Will and Testament, consisting of two pages, this _____ day of _____, _____.

_____

STATEMENT OF WITNESSES

We sign below as witnesses, declaring that the person who is making this will appears to be of sound mind and appears to be making this will freely and without duress, fraud, or undue influence and that the person making this will acknowledges that he or she has read, or has had it read to them, and understands the contents of this will.

_____   _____
(Print Name)   (Signature of Witness)

_____
(Address)

_____
(City)   (State)   (Zip)

_____   _____
(Print Name)   (Signature of Witness)

_____
(Address)

_____
(City)   (State)   (Zip)

Page 2 of ___ pages

Last Will and Testament
of

_____

I, _____ a resident of _____ County, Michigan, declare this to be my will, hereby revoking any prior wills and codicils.

FIRST: I direct that all my debts and funeral expenses be paid out of my estate as soon after my death as is practicable.

SECOND: I may leave a separate statement or list disposing of certain items of my tangible personal property. Any such statement or list in existence at the time of my death shall be determinative with respect to all items bequeathed therein.

THIRD: I give, devise, and bequeath all my estate, real, personal, and mixed, of whatever kind and wherever situated, of which I may die seized or possessed, or in which I may have any interest or over which I may have any power of appointment or testamentary disposition, as follows:
_____% to my spouse, _____ and
_____% to my children,

_____

_____,

in equal shares or to their lineal descendants per stirpes.

FOURTH: In the event that any beneficiary fails to survive me by thirty days, then this will shall take effect as if that person had predeceased me.

FIFTH: I hereby nominate, constitute, and appoint _____ as Personal Representative of this, my Last Will and Testament. In the event that such named person is unable or unwilling to serve at any time or for any reason, then I nominate, constitute, and appoint _____ as Personal Representative in the place and stead of the person first named herein. It is my will and I direct that my Personal Representative shall not be required to furnish a bond for the faithful performance of his or her duties in any jurisdiction, any provision of law to the contrary notwithstanding, and I give my Personal Representative full power to administer my estate, including the power to settle claims, pay debts, and sell, lease or exchange real and personal property without court order.

Testator Initials: _____

Page 1 of ___ pages

109

IN WITNESS WHEREOF I have signed and published this Last Will and Testament, consisting of two pages, this _____ day of _____, _____.

_____

STATEMENT OF WITNESSES

We sign below as witnesses, declaring that the person who is making this will appears to be of sound mind and appears to be making this will freely and without duress, fraud, or undue influence and that the person making this will acknowledges that he or she has read, or has had it read to them, and understands the contents of this will.

_____	_____
(Print Name)	(Signature of Witness)
_____	
(Address)	
_____	
(City) (State) (Zip)	

_____	_____
(Print Name)	(Signature of Witness)
_____	
(Address)	
_____	
(City) (State) (Zip)	

Page 2 of ___ pages

Last Will and Testament
of

_____

I, _____ a resident of _____ County, Michigan, declare this to be my will, hereby revoking any prior wills and codicils.

FIRST: I direct that all my debts and funeral expenses be paid out of my estate as soon after my death as is practicable.

SECOND: I may leave a separate statement or list disposing of certain items of my tangible personal property. Any such statement or list in existence at the time of my death shall be determinative with respect to all items bequeathed therein.

THIRD: I give, devise, and bequeath all my estate, real, personal, and mixed, of whatever kind and wherever situated, of which I may die seized or possessed, or in which I may have any interest or over which I may have any power of appointment or testamentary disposition, to my children _____

_____

_____,
plus any afterborn or adopted children in equal shares or to their lineal descendants per stirpes.

FOURTH: In the event that any beneficiary fails to survive me by thirty days, then this will shall take effect as if that person had predeceased me.

FIFTH: In the event any of my children have not attained the age of 18 years at the time of my death, I hereby nominate, constitute, and appoint _____ as guardian over the person and conservator over the estate of any of my children who have not reached the age of majority at the time of my death. In the event that said guardian/conservator is unable or unwilling to serve, then I nominate, constitute, and appoint _____ as guardian/conservator. Said guardian/conservator shall serve without bond or surety.

SIXTH: I hereby nominate, constitute, and appoint _____ as Personal Representative of this, my Last Will and Testament. In the event that such named person is unable or unwilling to serve at any time or for any reason, then I nominate, constitute, and appoint _____ as Personal Representative in the place and stead of the person first named herein. It is my will and I direct that my Personal

Testator Initials: _____

Page 1 of ___ pages

111

Representative shall not be required to furnish a bond for the faithful performance of his or her duties in any jurisdiction, any provision of law to the contrary notwithstanding, and I give my Personal Representative full power to administer my estate, including the power to settle claims, pay debts, and sell, lease or exchange real and personal property without court order.

IN WITNESS WHEREOF I have signed and published this Last Will and Testament, consisting of two pages, this _____ day of _____, _____.

_____

STATEMENT OF WITNESSES

We sign below as witnesses, declaring that the person who is making this will appears to be of sound mind and appears to be making this will freely and without duress, fraud, or undue influence and that the person making this will acknowledges that he or she has read, or has had it read to them, and understands the contents of this will.

_____   _____
           (Print Name)   (Signature of Witness)
_____
            (Address)
_____
(City)   (State)   (Zip)

_____   _____
           (Print Name)   (Signature of Witness)
_____
            (Address)
_____
(City)   (State)   (Zip)

Last Will and Testament
of

_____

I, _____ a resident of _____
County, Michigan, declare this to be my will, hereby revoking any prior wills and codicils.

FIRST: I direct that all my debts and funeral expenses be paid out of my estate as soon
after my death as is practicable.

SECOND: I may leave a separate statement or list disposing of certain items of my
tangible personal property. Any such statement or list in existence at the time of my death
shall be determinative with respect to all items bequeathed therein.

THIRD: I give, devise, and bequeath all my estate, real, personal, and mixed, of whatever kind and wherever situated, of which I may die seized or possessed, or in which I may
have any interest or over which I may have any power of appointment or testamentary disposition, to my children _____
_____
_____,
plus any afterborn or adopted children in equal shares or to their lineal descendants per
stirpes.

FOURTH: In the event that any beneficiary fails to survive me by thirty days, then
this will shall take effect as if that person had predeceased me.

FIFTH: In the event any of my children have not attained the age of 18 years at the
time of my death, I hereby nominate, constitute, and appoint _____
as guardian over the person of any of my children who have not reached the age of majority
at the time of my death. In the event that said guardian is unable or unwilling to serve, then
I nominate, constitute, and appoint _____ as guardian.
Said guardian shall serve without bond or surety.

SIXTH: In the event any of my children have not attained the age of 18 years at the
time of my death, I hereby nominate, constitute, and appoint _____
as conservator over the property of any of my children who have not reached the age of
majority at the time of my death. In the event that said conservator is unable or unwilling to
serve, then I nominate, constitute, and appoint _____
as conservator. Said conservator shall serve without bond or surety.

Testator Initials: _____

SEVENTH: I hereby nominate, constitute, and appoint _____ as Personal Representative of this, my Last Will and Testament. In the event that such named person is unable or unwilling to serve at any time or for any reason, then I nominate, constitute, and appoint _____ as Personal Representative in the place and stead of the person first named herein. It is my will and I direct that my Personal Representative shall not be required to furnish a bond for the faithful performance of his or her duties in any jurisdiction, any provision of law to the contrary notwithstanding, and I give my Personal Representative full power to administer my estate, including the power to settle claims, pay debts, and sell, lease or exchange real and personal property without court order.

IN WITNESS WHEREOF I have signed and published this Last Will and Testament, consisting of two pages, this _____ day of _____, _____.

_____

STATEMENT OF WITNESSES

We sign below as witnesses, declaring that the person who is making this will appears to be of sound mind and appears to be making this will freely and without duress, fraud, or undue influence and that the person making this will acknowledges that he or she has read, or has had it read to them, and understands the contents of this will.

_____   _____
(Print Name)   (Signature of Witness)

_____
(Address)

_____   _____   _____
(City)   (State)   (Zip)

_____   _____
(Print Name)   (Signature of Witness)

_____
(Address)

_____   _____   _____
(City)   (State)   (Zip)

Last Will and Testament

I, _____ a resident of _____ County, Michigan, declare this to be my will, hereby revoking any prior wills and codicils.

FIRST: I direct that all my debts and funeral expenses be paid out of my estate as soon after my death as is practicable.

SECOND: I may leave a separate statement or list disposing of certain items of my tangible personal property. Any such statement or list in existence at the time of my death shall be determinative with respect to all items bequeathed therein.

THIRD: I give, devise, and bequeath all my estate, real, personal, and mixed, of whatever kind and wherever situated, of which I may die seized or possessed, or in which I may have any interest or over which I may have any power of appointment or testamentary disposition, to my children _____

_____

_____,

plus any afterborn or adopted children in equal shares or to their lineal descendants per stirpes.

FOURTH: In the event that any beneficiary fails to survive me by thirty days, then this will shall take effect as if that person had predeceased me.

FIFTH: In the event that any of my children have not reached the age of _____ years at the time of my death, then the share of any such child shall be held in a separate trust by _____ for such child.

The trustee shall use the income and that part of the principal of the trust as is, in the trustee's sole discretion, necessary or desirable to provide proper housing, medical care, food, clothing, entertainment and education for the trust beneficiary, considering the beneficiary's other resources. Any income that is not distributed shall be added to the principal. Additionally, the trustee shall have all powers conferred by the law of the state having jurisdiction over this trust, as well as the power to pay from the assets of the trust reasonable fees necessary to administer the trust.

The trust shall terminate when the child reaches the age specified above and the remaining assets distributed to the child, unless they have been exhausted sooner. In the event the child dies prior to the termination of the trust, then the assets shall pass to the estate of the child. The interests of the beneficiary under this trust shall not be assignable and shall be free from the claims of creditors to the full extent allowed by law.

In the event the said trustee is unable or unwilling to serve for any reason, then I nominate, constitute, and appoint _____ as alternate trustee. No bond shall be required of either trustee in any jurisdiction and this trust shall be administered without court supervision as allowed by law.

Testator Initials: _____

SIXTH: In the event any of my children have not attained the age of 18 years at the time of my death, I hereby nominate, constitute, and appoint _____ as guardian over the person of any of my children who have not reached the age of majority at the time of my death. In the event that said guardian is unable or unwilling to serve, then I nominate, constitute, and appoint _____ as guardian. Said guardian shall serve without bond or surety.

SEVENTH: I hereby nominate, constitute, and appoint _____ as Personal Representative of this, my Last Will and Testament. In the event that such named person is unable or unwilling to serve at any time or for any reason, then I nominate, constitute, and appoint _____ as Personal Representative in the place and stead of the person first named herein. It is my will and I direct that my Personal Representative shall not be required to furnish a bond for the faithful performance of his or her duties in any jurisdiction, any provision of law to the contrary notwithstanding, and I give my Personal Representative full power to administer my estate, including the power to settle claims, pay debts, and sell, lease or exchange real and personal property without court order.

IN WITNESS WHEREOF I have signed and published this Last Will and Testament, consisting of two pages, this _____ day of _____, _____.

_____

STATEMENT OF WITNESSES

We sign below as witnesses, declaring that the person who is making this will appears to be of sound mind and appears to be making this will freely and without duress, fraud, or undue influence and that the person making this will acknowledges that he or she has read, or has had it read to them, and understands the contents of this will.

_____	_____
(Signature of Witness)	(Signature of Witness)
_____	_____
(Print Name)	(Print Name)
_____	_____
(Address)	(Address)
_____	_____
(City) (State) (Zip)	(City) (State) (Zip)

Last Will and Testament

I, _____ a resident of _____ County, Michigan, declare this to be my will, hereby revoking any prior wills and codicils.

FIRST: I direct that all my debts and funeral expenses be paid out of my estate as soon after my death as is practicable.

SECOND: I may leave a separate statement or list disposing of certain items of my tangible personal property. Any such statement or list in existence at the time of my death shall be determinative with respect to all items bequeathed therein.

THIRD: I give, devise, and bequeath all my estate, real, personal, and mixed, of whatever kind and wherever situated, of which I may die seized or possessed, or in which I may have any interest or over which I may have any power of appointment or testamentary disposition, to my children _____ _____, in equal shares, or their lineal descendants per stirpes.

FOURTH: In the event that any beneficiary fails to survive me by thirty days, then this will shall take effect as if that person had predeceased me.

FIFTH: I hereby nominate, constitute, and appoint _____ as Personal Representative of this, my Last Will and Testament. In the event that such named person is unable or unwilling to serve at any time or for any reason, then I nominate, constitute, and appoint _____ as Personal Representative in the place and stead of the person first named herein. It is my will and I direct that my Personal Representative shall not be required to furnish a bond for the faithful performance of his or her duties in any jurisdiction, any provision of law to the contrary notwithstanding, and I give my Personal Representative full power to administer my estate, including the power to settle claims, pay debts, and sell, lease or exchange real and personal property without court order.

IN WITNESS WHEREOF I have signed and published this Last Will and Testament, consisting of two pages, this _____ day of _____, _____.

_____

STATEMENT OF WITNESSES

We sign below as witnesses, declaring that the person who is making this will appears to be of sound mind and appears to be making this will freely and without duress, fraud, or undue influence and that the person making this will acknowledges that he or she has read, or has had it read to them, and understands the contents of this will.

_____			_____		
(Signature of Witness)			(Signature of Witness)		
_____			_____		
(Print Name)			(Print Name)		
_____			_____		
(Address)			(Address)		
_____	_____	_____	_____	_____	_____
(City)	(State)	(Zip)	(City)	(State)	(Zip)

117

This page intentionally left blank.

Last Will and Testament

I, _____ a resident of _____ County, Michigan, declare this to be my will, hereby revoking any prior wills and codicils.

FIRST: I direct that all my debts and funeral expenses be paid out of my estate as soon after my death as is practicable.

SECOND: I may leave a separate statement or list disposing of certain items of my tangible personal property. Any such statement or list in existence at the time of my death shall be determinative with respect to all items bequeathed therein.

THIRD: I give, devise, and bequeath all my estate, real, personal, and mixed, of whatever kind and wherever situated, of which I may die seized or possessed, or in which I may have any interest or over which I may have any power of appointment or testamentary disposition, to my children_____ _____, in equal shares, or their lineal descendants per capita.

FOURTH: In the event that any beneficiary fails to survive me by thirty days, then this will shall take effect as if that person had predeceased me.

FIFTH: I hereby nominate, constitute, and appoint _____ as Personal Representative of this, my Last Will and Testament. In the event that such named person is unable or unwilling to serve at any time or for any reason, then I nominate, constitute, and appoint _____ as Personal Representative in the place and stead of the person first named herein. It is my will and I direct that my Personal Representative shall not be required to furnish a bond for the faithful performance of his or her duties in any jurisdiction, any provision of law to the contrary notwithstanding, and I give my Personal Representative full power to administer my estate, including the power to settle claims, pay debts, and sell, lease or exchange real and personal property without court order.

IN WITNESS WHEREOF I have signed and published this Last Will and Testament, consisting of two pages, this _____ day of _____, _____.

_____

STATEMENT OF WITNESSES

We sign below as witnesses, declaring that the person who is making this will appears to be of sound mind and appears to be making this will freely and without duress, fraud, or undue influence and that the person making this will acknowledges that he or she has read, or has had it read to them, and understands the contents of this will.

_____	_____
(Signature of Witness)	(Signature of Witness)
_____	_____
(Print Name)	(Print Name)
_____	_____
(Address)	(Address)
_____	_____
(City) (State) (Zip)	(City) (State) (Zip)

119

This page intentionally left blank.

Last Will and Testament
of

_____

I, _____ a resident of _____ County, Michigan, declare this to be my will, hereby revoking any prior wills and codicils.

FIRST: I direct that all my debts and funeral expenses be paid out of my estate as soon after my death as is practicable.

SECOND: I may leave a separate statement or list disposing of certain items of my tangible personal property. Any such statement or list in existence at the time of my death shall be determinative with respect to all items bequeathed therein.

THIRD: I give, devise, and bequeath all my estate, real, personal, and mixed, of whatever kind and wherever situated, of which I may die seized or possessed, or in which I may have any interest or over which I may have any power of appointment or testamentary disposition, to the following:

_____

_____

_____

_____

_____

_____,

or to the survivor of them.

FOURTH: In the event that any beneficiary fails to survive me by thirty days, then this will shall take effect as if that person had predeceased me.

FIFTH: I hereby nominate, constitute, and appoint _____ as Personal Representative of this, my Last Will and Testament. In the event that such named person is unable or unwilling to serve at any time or for any reason, then I nominate, constitute, and appoint _____ as Personal Representative in the place and stead of the person first named herein. It is my will and I direct that my Personal Representative shall not be required to furnish a bond for the faithful performance of his or her duties in any jurisdiction, any provision of law to the contrary notwithstanding, and I give my Personal Representative full power to administer my estate, including the power to settle claims, pay debts, and sell, lease or exchange real and personal property without court order.

Testator Initials: _____

Page 1 of ___ pages

IN WITNESS WHEREOF I have signed and published this Last Will and Testament, consisting of two pages, this _____ day of _____, _____.

_____

STATEMENT OF WITNESSES

We sign below as witnesses, declaring that the person who is making this will appears to be of sound mind and appears to be making this will freely and without duress, fraud, or undue influence and that the person making this will acknowledges that he or she has read, or has had it read to them, and understands the contents of this will.

_____	_____
(Print Name)	(Signature of Witness)

_____
(Address)

(City)	(State)	(Zip)

_____	_____
(Print Name)	(Signature of Witness)

_____
(Address)

(City)	(State)	(Zip)

Page 2 of ___ pages

Last Will and Testament
of

_____

I, _____ a resident of _____ County, Michigan, declare this to be my will, hereby revoking any prior wills and codicils.

FIRST: I direct that all my debts and funeral expenses be paid out of my estate as soon after my death as is practicable.

SECOND: I may leave a separate statement or list disposing of certain items of my tangible personal property. Any such statement or list in existence at the time of my death shall be determinative with respect to all items bequeathed therein.

THIRD: I give, devise, and bequeath all my estate, real, personal, and mixed, of whatever kind and wherever situated, of which I may die seized or possessed, or in which I may have any interest or over which I may have any power of appointment or testamentary disposition, to the following:

_____

_____

_____

_____

_____ ,

in equal shares, or their lineal descendants per stirpes.

FOURTH: In the event that any beneficiary fails to survive me by thirty days, then this will shall take effect as if that person had predeceased me.

FIFTH: I hereby nominate, constitute, and appoint _____ as Personal Representative of this, my Last Will and Testament. In the event that such named person is unable or unwilling to serve at any time or for any reason, then I nominate, constitute, and appoint _____ as Personal Representative in the place and stead of the person first named herein. It is my will and I direct that my Personal Representative shall not be required to furnish a bond for the faithful performance of his or her duties in any jurisdiction, any provision of law to the contrary notwithstanding, and I give my Personal Representative full power to administer my estate, including the power to settle claims, pay debts, and sell, lease or exchange real and personal property without court order.

Testator Initials: _____

Page 1 of ___ pages

123

IN WITNESS WHEREOF I have signed and published this Last Will and Testament, consisting of two pages, this _____ day of _____, _____.

_____

STATEMENT OF WITNESSES

We sign below as witnesses, declaring that the person who is making this will appears to be of sound mind and appears to be making this will freely and without duress, fraud, or undue influence and that the person making this will acknowledges that he or she has read, or has had it read to them, and understands the contents of this will.

_____	_____
(Print Name)	(Signature of Witness)
_____	
(Address)	
_____ _____ _____	
(City) (State) (Zip)	

_____	_____
(Print Name)	(Signature of Witness)
_____	
(Address)	
_____ _____ _____	
(City) (State) (Zip)	

STATE OF MICHIGAN

COUNTY OF _____

    I, _____, the testator, sign my name to this document on _____, _____. I have taken an oath, administered by the officer whose signature and seal appear on this document, swearing that the statements in this document are true. I declare to that officer that this document is my will; that I sign it willingly or willingly direct another to sign for me; that I execute it as my voluntary act for the purposes expressed in this will; and that I am 18 years of age or older, of sound mind, and under no constraint or undue influence.

_____
                     (Signature) Testator

We, _____ and _____, the witnesses, sign our names to this document and have taken an oath, administered by the officer whose signature and seal appear on this document, to swear that all of the following statements are true: the individual signing this document as the testator executes the document as his or her will, signs it willingly or willingly directs another to sign for him or her, and executes it as his or her voluntary act for the purposes expressed in this will; each of us, in the testator's presence, signs this will as witness to the testator's signing; and, to the best of our knowledge, the testator is 18 years of age or older, of sound mind, and under no constraint or undue influence.

_____
                     Signature (Witness)

_____
                     (Signature) Witness

The State of _____
County of _____

Sworn to and signed in my presence by _____, the testator, and sworn to and signed in my presence by _____ and _____ , witnesses, on_____, _____ .month/day/year

_____
                 (SEAL) Signed
Notary Public
My Commission Expires:
                Page ___ of ___ pages

This page intentionally left blank.

Codicil to the Will of

_____

I, _____, a resident of _____
County, Michigan, declare this to be the first codicil to my Last Will and Testament dated
_____, _____.

FIRST: I hereby revoke the clause of my Will which reads as follows: _____
_____
_____
_____.

SECOND: I hereby add the following clause to my Will: _____
_____
_____
_____.

THIRD: In all other respects I hereby confirm and republish my Last Will and
Testament dated _____, _____.

IN WITNESS WHEREOF, I have signed and published the foregoing instrument as
and for a codicil to my Last Will and Testament, this _____ day of _____,
_____.

_____

STATEMENT OF WITNESSES

We sign below as witnesses, declaring that the person who is making this will appears to be of
sound mind and appears to be making this will freely and without duress, fraud, or undue influence
and that the person making this will acknowledges that he or she has read, or has had it read to them,
and understands the contents of this will.

_____	_____
(Signature of Witness)	(Signature of Witness)
_____	_____
(Print Name)	(Print Name)
_____	_____
(Address)	(Address)
_____	_____
(City) (State) (Zip)	(City) (State) (Zip)

This page intentionally left blank.

STATE OF MICHIGAN

COUNTY OF _____

      I, _____, the testator, sign my name to this document on _____, _____. I have taken an oath, administered by the officer whose signature and seal appear on this document, swearing that the statements in this document are true. I declare to that officer that this document is a codicil to my will; that I sign it willingly or willingly direct another to sign for me; that I execute it as my voluntary act for the purposes expressed in this codicil; and that I am 18 years of age or older, of sound mind, and under no constraint or undue influence.

_____
(Signature) Testator

We, _____ and _____, the witnesses, sign our names to this document and have taken an oath, administered by the officer whose signature and seal appear on this document, to swear that all of the following statements are true: the individual signing this document as the testator executes the document as a codicil to his or her will, signs it willingly or willingly directs another to sign for him or her, and executes it as his or her voluntary act for the purposes expressed in this codicil; each of us, in the testator's presence, signs this codicil as witness to the testator's signing; and, to the best of our knowledge, the testator is 18 years of age or older, of sound mind, and under no constraint or undue influence.

_____
(Signature) Witness

_____
(Signature) Witness

The State of _____
County of _____
Sworn to and signed in my presence by _____, the testator, and sworn to and signed in my presence by _____ and _____ , witnesses, on _____, _____ month/day/year

_____
(SEAL) Signed
Notary Public
My Commission Expires:

This page intentionally left blank.

Designation of Patient Advocate and Living Will

I, _____, appoint
_____, whose address is
_____ and whose
telephone number is _____, as my patient advocate pursuant to M.S.A.
§27.5496; M.C.L.A. §700.496. I appoint _____,
whose address is _____ and whose
telephone number is _____, as my alternate patient advocate in the event my
patient advocate designated above does not accept the appointment, is incapacitated, or is removed.
I authorize my patient advocate to make health care decisions for me when I am incapable of making my own heath care decisions, including decisions to withhold or withdraw medical treatment, even if such withholding or withdrawal could or would allow me to die. I understand the consequences of appointing a patient advocate.

I direct that my agent comply with the following instructions or limitations:
_____
_____.

I also direct that my patient advocate have authority to make decisions regarding the enforcement of my intentions regarding life-prolonging procedures as stated below:

I, _____, being of
sound mind willfully and voluntarily make known my desire that my dying shall not be artificially prolonged under the circumstances set forth below, do hereby declare:

If I should have an incurable or irreversible condition that will cause my death within a relatively short time, and if I am unable to make decisions regarding my medical treatment, I direct my attending physician to withhold or withdraw procedures that merely prolong the dying process and are not necessary to my comfort, or to alleviate pain.

This authorization [check only one box] ❑ includes   ❑ does not include the withholding or withdrawal of artificial feeding and hydration.

Signed this _____ day of _____, _____.

_____
Signature
Address:_____
_____

The declarant is personally known to me and voluntarily signed this document in my presence.

Witness:_____   Witness:_____
Name:_____   Name:_____
Address:_____   Address:_____
_____   _____

Acceptance of Patient Advocate

I HEREBY accept the appointment as patient advocate and understand that:

(a)   This designation shall not become effective unless the patient is unable to participate in medical decisions.

(b)   A patient advocate shall not exercise powers concerning the patient's care, custody, and medical treatment that the patient, if the patient were able to participate in the decision, could not have exercised on his or her own behalf.

(c)   This designation cannot be used to make a medical treatment decision to withhold or withdraw treatment from a patient who is pregnant that would result in the pregnant patient's death.

(d)   A patient advocate may make a decision to withhold or withdraw treatment which would allow a patient to die only if the patient has expressed in a clear and convincing manner that the patient advocate is authorized to make such a decision, and that the patient acknowledges that such a decision could or would allow the patient's death.

(e)   A patient advocate shall not receive compensation for the performance of his or her authority, rights, and responsibilities, but a patient advocate may be reimbursed for actual and necessary expenses incurred in the performance of his or her authority, rights, and responsibilities.

(f)   A patient advocate shall act in accordance with the standards of care applicable to fiduciaries when acting for the patient and shall act consistent with the patient's best interests. The known desires of the patient expressed or evidenced while the patient is able to participate in medical treatment decisions are presumed to be in the patient's best interests.

(g)   A patient may revoke his or her designation at any time and in any manner sufficient to communicate an intent to revoke.

(h)   A patient advocate may revoke his or her acceptance to the designation at any time and in any manner sufficient to communicate an intent to revoke.

(i)   A patient admitted to a health facility or agency has the rights enumerated in section 20201 of the public health code, Act No. 368 of the Public Acts of 1978, being section 33.20201 of the Michigan Compiled Laws.

Date: _____

_____
Signature

UNIFORM DONOR CARD

The undersigned hereby makes this anatomical gift, if medically acceptable, to take effect on death. The words and marks below indicate my desires:

I give: (a) _____ any needed organs or parts;

(b) _____ only the following organs or parts

_____

for the purpose of transplantation, therapy, medical research, or education;

(c) _____ my body for anatomical study if needed.

Limitations or special wishes, if any:

_____

_____

Signed by the donor and the following witnesses in the presence of each other:

_____   _____
Signature of Donor   Date of birth

_____   _____
Date signed   City & State

_____   _____
Witness   Witness

_____   _____
Address   Address

UNIFORM DONOR CARD

The undersigned hereby makes this anatomical gift, if medically acceptable, to take effect on death. The words and marks below indicate my desires:

I give: (a) _____ any needed organs or parts;

(b) _____ only the following organs or parts

_____

for the purpose of transplantation, therapy, medical research, or education;

(c) _____ my body for anatomical study if needed.

Limitations or special wishes, if any:

_____

_____

Signed by the donor and the following witnesses in the presence of each other:

_____   _____
Signature of Donor   Date of birth

_____   _____
Date signed   City & State

_____   _____
Witness   Witness

_____   _____
Address   Address

UNIFORM DONOR CARD

The undersigned hereby makes this anatomical gift, if medically acceptable, to take effect on death. The words and marks below indicate my desires:

I give: (a) _____ any needed organs or parts;

(b) _____ only the following organs or parts

_____

for the purpose of transplantation, therapy, medical research, or education;

(c) _____ my body for anatomical study if needed.

Limitations or special wishes, if any:

_____

Signed by the donor and the following witnesses in the presence of each other:

_____   _____
Signature of Donor   Date of birth

_____   _____
Date signed   City & State

_____   _____
Witness   Witness

_____   _____
Address   Address

UNIFORM DONOR CARD

The undersigned hereby makes this anatomical gift, if medically acceptable, to take effect on death. The words and marks below indicate my desires:

I give: (a) _____ any needed organs or parts;

(b) _____ only the following organs or parts

_____

for the purpose of transplantation, therapy, medical research, or education;

(c) _____ my body for anatomical study if needed.

Limitations or special wishes, if any:

_____

Signed by the donor and the following witnesses in the presence of each other:

_____   _____
Signature of Donor   Date of birth

_____   _____
Date signed   City & State

_____   _____
Witness   Witness

_____   _____
Address   Address

One of these cards should be cut out and carried in your wallet or purse.

This page intentionally left blank.

Self-Proving Affidavit

I, _____, the testator, sign my name to this document on _____, _____. I have taken an oath, administered by the officer whose signature and seal appear on this document, swearing that the statements in this document are true. I declare to that officer that this document is a codicil to my will; that I sign it willingly or willingly direct another to sign for me; that I execute it as my voluntary act for the purposes expressed in this codicil; and that I am 18 years of age or older, of sound mind, and under no constraint or undue influence.

_____
(Signature) Testator

We, _____ and _____, the witnesses, sign our names to this document and have taken an oath, administered by the officer whose signature and seal appear on this document, to swear that all of the following statements are true: the individual signing this document as the testator executes the document as a codicil to his or her will, signs it willingly or willingly directs another to sign for him or her, and executes it as his or her voluntary act for the purposes expressed in this codicil; each of us, in the testator's presence, signs this codicil as witness to the testator's signing; and, to the best of our knowledge, the testator is 18 years of age or older, of sound mind, and under no constraint or undue influence.

_____
(Signature) Witness

_____
(Signature) Witness

The State of _____

County of _____

Sworn to and signed in my presence by _____, the testator, and sworn to and signed in my presence by_____ and _____ , witnesses, on _____, _____ month/day/year

_____
(SEAL) Signed

Notary Public

My Commission Expires:

The State of _____

County of _____

We, _____, _____, and _____, the testator and the witnesses, respectively, whose names are signed to the attached will, sign this document and have taken an oath, administered by the officer whose signature and seal appear on this document, to swear that all of the following statements are true: the individual signing this document as the will's testator executed the will as his or her will, signed it willingly or willingly directed another to sign for him or her, and executed it as his or her voluntary act for the purposes expressed in the will; each witness, in the testator's presence, signed the will as witness to the testator's signing; and, to the best of the witnesses' knowledge, the testator, at the time of the will's execution, was 18 years of age or older, of sound mind, and under no constraint or undue influence..

_____

(Signature) Testator

_____   _____

(Signature) Witness   (Signature) Witness

Sworn to and signed in my presence by _____, the testator, and sworn to and signed in my presence by _____ and _____, witnesses, on _____, _____ . month/day/year

_____

(SEAL) (Signed)

Notary Public

My Commission Expires:

INDEX

SPHINX® PUBLISHING'S NATIONAL TITLES

Valid in All 50 States

LEGAL SURVIVAL IN BUSINESS

The Complete Book of Corporate Forms	$24.95
How to Form a Delaware Corporation from Any State	$24.95
How to Form a Limited Liability Company	$22.95
Incorporate in Nevada from Any State	$24.95
How to Form a Nonprofit Corporation	$24.95
How to Form Your Own Corporation (3E)	$24.95
How to Form Your Own Partnership	$22.95
How to Register Your Own Copyright (3E)	$21.95
How to Register Your Own Trademark (3E)	$21.95
Most Valuable Business Legal Forms You'll Ever Need (3E)	$21.95

LEGAL SURVIVAL IN COURT

Crime Victim's Guide to Justice (2E)	$21.95
Grandparents' Rights (3E)	$24.95
Help Your Lawyer Win Your Case (2E)	$14.95
Jurors' Rights (2E)	$12.95
Legal Research Made Easy (2E)	$16.95
Winning Your Personal Injury Claim (2E)	$24.95
Your Rights When You Owe Too Much	$16.95

LEGAL SURVIVAL IN REAL ESTATE

Essential Guide to Real Estate Contracts	$18.95
Essential Guide to Real Estate Leases	$18.95
How to Buy a Condominium or Townhome (2E)	$19.95

LEGAL SURVIVAL IN PERSONAL AFFAIRS

Cómo Hacer su Propio Testamento	$16.95
Guía de Inmigración a Estados Unidos (3E)	$24.95
Guía de Justicia para Víctimas del Crimen	$21.95
Cómo Solicitar su Propio Divorcio	$24.95
How to File Your Own Bankruptcy (5E)	$21.95
How to File Your Own Divorce (4E)	$24.95
How to Make Your Own Will (2E)	$16.95
How to Write Your Own Living Will (2E)	$16.95
How to Write Your Own Premarital Agreement (3E)	$24.95
How to Win Your Unemployment Compensation Claim	$21.95
Living Trusts and Simple Ways to Avoid Probate (2E)	$22.95
Manual de Beneficios para el Seguro Social	$18.95
Most Valuable Personal Legal Forms You'll Ever Need	$24.95
Neighbor v. Neighbor (2E)	$16.95
The Nanny and Domestic Help Legal Kit	$22.95
The Power of Attorney Handbook (3E)	$19.95
Repair Your Own Credit and Deal with Debt	$18.95
The Social Security Benefits Handbook (3E)	$18.95
Unmarried Parents' Rights	$19.95
U.S.A. Immigration Guide (3E)	$19.95
Your Right to Child Custody, Visitation and Support (2E)	$24.95

Legal Survival Guides are directly available from Sourcebooks, Inc., or from your local bookstores.
Prices are subject to change without notice.

For credit card orders call 1–800–432–7444, write P.O. Box 4410, Naperville, IL 60567-4410
or fax 630-961-2168

SPHINX® PUBLISHING ORDER FORM

<table>
<tr><td colspan="2">BILL TO:</td><td colspan="3">SHIP TO:</td></tr>
<tr><td colspan="2"></td><td colspan="3"></td></tr>
<tr><td colspan="2"></td><td colspan="3"></td></tr>
<tr><td>Phone #</td><td>Terms</td><td>F.O.B. Chicago, IL</td><td>Ship Date</td></tr>
</table>

Charge my: ☐ VISA   ☐ MasterCard   ☐ American Express

☐ **Money Order or Personal Check**

Credit Card Number [ ][ ][ ][ ][ ][ ][ ][ ][ ][ ][ ][ ][ ][ ][ ][ ]   **Expiration Date**

Qty	ISBN	Title	Retail	Ext.
		SPHINX PUBLISHING NATIONAL TITLES		
	1-57248-148-X	Cómo Hacer su Propio Testamento	$16.95	
	1-57248-147-1	Cómo Solicitar su Propio Divorcio	$24.95	
	1-57248-166-8	The Complete Book of Corporate Forms	$24.95	
	1-57248-163-3	Crime Victim's Guide to Justice (2E)	$21.95	
	1-57248-159-5	Essential Guide to Real Estate Contracts	$18.95	
	1-57248-160-9	Essential Guide to Real Estate Leases	$18.95	
	1-57248-139-0	Grandparents' Rights (3E)	$24.95	
	1-57248-188-9	Guía de Inmigración a Estados Unidos (3E)	$24.95	
	1-57248-187-0	Guía de Justicia para Víctimas del Crimen	$21.95	
	1-57248-103-X	Help Your Lawyer Win Your Case (2E)	$14.95	
	1-57248-164-1	How to Buy a Condominium or Townhome (2E)	$19.95	
	1-57248-191-9	How to File Your Own Bankruptcy (5E)	$21.95	
	1-57248-132-3	How to File Your Own Divorce (4E)	$24.95	
	1-57248-100-5	How to Form a DE Corporation from Any State	$24.95	
	1-57248-083-1	How to Form a Limited Liability Company	$22.95	
	1-57248-099-8	How to Form a Nonprofit Corporation	$24.95	
	1-57248-133-1	How to Form Your Own Corporation (3E)	$24.95	
	1-57071-343-X	How to Form Your Own Partnership	$22.95	
	1-57248-119-6	How to Make Your Own Will (2E)	$16.95	
	1-57248-124-2	How to Register Your Own Copyright (3E)	$21.95	
	1-57248-104-8	How to Register Your Own Trademark (3E)	$21.95	
	1-57071-349-9	How to Win Your Unemployment Compensation Claim	$21.95	
	1-57248-118-8	How to Write Your Own Living Will (2E)	$16.95	
	1-57248-156-0	How to Write Your Own Premarital Agreement (3E)	$24.95	
	1-57248-158-7	Incorporate in Nevada from Any State	$24.95	
	1-57071-333-2	Jurors' Rights (2E)	$12.95	
	1-57071-400-2	Legal Research Made Easy (2E)	$16.95	
	1-57071-336-7	Living Trusts and Simple Ways to Avoid Probate (2E)	$22.95	

Qty	ISBN	Title	Retail	Ext.
	1-57248-186-2	Manual de Beneficios para el Seguro Social	$18.95	
	1-57248-167-6	Most Valuable Bus. Legal Forms You'll Ever Need (3E)	$21.95	
	1-57248-130-7	Most Valuable Personal Legal Forms You'll Ever Need	$24.95	
	1-57248-098-X	The Nanny and Domestic Help Legal Kit	$22.95	
	1-57248-089-0	Neighbor v. Neighbor (2E)	$16.95	
	1-57071-348-0	The Power of Attorney Handbook (3E)	$19.95	
	1-57248-149-8	Repair Your Own Credit and Deal with Debt	$18.95	
	1-57248-168-4	The Social Security Benefits Handbook (3E)	$18.95	
	1-57071-399-5	Unmarried Parents' Rights	$19.95	
	1-57071-354-5	U.S.A. Immigration Guide (3E)	$19.95	
	1-57248-138-2	Winning Your Personal Injury Claim (2E)	$24.95	
	1-57248-162-5	Your Right to Child Custody, Visitation and Support (2E)	$24.95	
	1-57248-157-9	Your Rights When You Owe Too Much	$16.95	
		CALIFORNIA TITLES		
	1-57248-150-1	CA Power of Attorney Handbook (2E)	$18.95	
	1-57248-151-X	How to File for Divorce in CA (3E)	$26.95	
	1-57071-356-1	How to Make a CA Will	$16.95	
	1-57248-145-5	How to Probate and Settle an Estate in California	$26.95	
	1-57248-146-3	How to Start a Business in CA	$18.95	
	1-57071-358-8	How to Win in Small Claims Court in CA	$16.95	
	1-57071-359-6	Landlords' Rights and Duties in CA	$21.95	
		FLORIDA TITLES		
	1-57071-363-4	Florida Power of Attorney Handbook (2E)	$16.95	
	1-57248-176-5	How to File for Divorce in FL (7E)	$26.95	
	1-57248-177-3	How to Form a Corporation in FL (5E)	$24.95	
	1-57248-086-6	How to Form a Limited Liability Co. in FL	$22.95	
	1-57071-401-0	How to Form a Partnership in FL	$22.95	
	1-57248-113-7	How to Make a FL Will (6E)	$16.95	

Form Continued on Following Page   **SUBTOTAL**

To order, call Sourcebooks at 1-800-432-7444 or FAX (630) 961-2168 (Bookstores, libraries, wholesalers—please call for discount)

Prices are subject to change without notice.

SPHINX® PUBLISHING ORDER FORM

Qty	ISBN	Title	Retail	Ext.
_____	1-57248-088-2	How to Modify Your FL Divorce Judgment (4E)	$24.95	_____
_____	1-57248-144-7	How to Probate and Settle an Estate in FL (4E)	$26.95	_____
_____	1-57248-081-5	How to Start a Business in FL (5E)	$16.95	_____
_____	1-57071-362-6	How to Win in Small Claims Court in FL (6E)	$16.95	_____
_____	1-57248-123-4	Landlords' Rights and Duties in FL (8E)	$21.95	_____
		GEORGIA TITLES		
_____	1-57248-137-4	How to File for Divorce in GA (4E)	$21.95	_____
_____	1-57248-075-0	How to Make a GA Will (3E)	$16.95	_____
_____	1-57248-140-4	How to Start a Business in Georgia (2E)	$16.95	_____
		ILLINOIS TITLES		
_____	1-57071-405-3	How to File for Divorce in IL (2E)	$21.95	_____
_____	1-57248-170-6	How to Make an IL Will (3E)	$16.95	_____
_____	1-57071-416-9	How to Start a Business in IL (2E)	$18.95	_____
_____	1-57248-078-5	Landlords' Rights & Duties in IL	$21.95	_____
		MASSACHUSETTS TITLES		
_____	1-57248-128-5	How to File for Divorce in MA (3E)	$24.95	_____
_____	1-57248-115-3	How to Form a Corporation in MA	$24.95	_____
_____	1-57248-108-0	How to Make a MA Will (2E)	$16.95	_____
_____	1-57248-106-4	How to Start a Business in MA (2E)	$18.95	_____
_____	1-57248-107-2	Landlords' Rights and Duties in MA (2E)	$21.95	_____
		MICHIGAN TITLES		
_____	1-57071-409-6	How to File for Divorce in MI (2E)	$21.95	_____
_____	1-57248-182-X	How to Make a MI Will (3E)	$16.95	_____
_____	1-57248-183-8	How to Start a Business in MI (3E)	$18.95	_____
		MINNESOTA TITLES		
_____	1-57248-142-0	How to File for Divorce in MN	$21.95	_____
_____	1-57248-179-X	How to Form a Corporation in MN	$24.95	_____
_____	1-57248-178-1	How to Make a MN Will (2E)	$16.95	_____
		NEW YORK TITLES		
_____	1-57248-141-2	How to File for Divorce in NY (2E)	$26.95	_____
_____	1-57248-105-6	How to Form a Corporation in NY	$24.95	_____
_____	1-57248-095-5	How to Make a NY Will (2E)	$16.95	_____
_____	1-57071-185-2	How to Start a Business in NY	$18.95	_____
_____	1-57071-187-9	How to Win in Small Claims Court in NY	$16.95	_____
_____	1-57071-186-0	Landlords' Rights and Duties in NY	$21.95	_____

Qty	ISBN	Title	Retail	Ext.
_____	1-57071-188-7	New York Power of Attorney Handbook	$19.95	_____
_____	1-57248-122-6	Tenants' Rights in NY	$21.95	_____
		NORTH CAROLINA TITLES		
_____	1-57248-185-4	How to File for Divorce in NC (3E)	$22.95	_____
_____	1-57248-129-3	How to Make a NC Will (3E)	$16.95	_____
_____	1-57248-184-6	How to Start a Business in NC (3E)	$18.95	_____
_____	1-57248-091-2	Landlords' Rights & Duties in NC	$21.95	_____
		OHIO TITLES		
_____	1-57248-190-0	How to File for Divorce in OH (2E)	$24.95	_____
_____	1-57248-174-9	How to Form a Corporation in OH	$24.95	_____
_____	1-57248-173-0	How to Make an OH Will	$16.95	_____
		PENNSYLVANIA TITLES		
_____	1-57248-127-7	How to File for Divorce in PA (2E)	$24.95	_____
_____	1-57248-094-7	How to Make a PA Will (2E)	$16.95	_____
_____	1-57248-112-9	How to Start a Business in PA (2E)	$18.95	_____
_____	1-57071-179-8	Landlords' Rights and Duties in PA	$19.95	_____
		TEXAS TITLES		
_____	1-57248-171-4	Child Custody, Visitation, and Support in TX	$22.95	_____
_____	1-57248-172-2	How to File for Divorce in TX (3E)	$24.95	_____
_____	1-57248-114-5	How to Form a Corporation in TX (2E)	$24.95	_____
_____	1-57071-417-7	How to Make a TX Will (2E)	$16.95	_____
_____	1-57071-418-5	How to Probate an Estate in TX (2E)	$22.95	_____
_____	1-57071-365-0	How to Start a Business in TX (2E)	$18.95	_____
_____	1-57248-111-0	How to Win in Small Claims Court in TX (2E)	$16.95	_____
_____	1-57248-110-2	Landlords' Rights and Duties in TX (2E)	$21.95	_____

SUBTOTAL THIS PAGE _____

SUBTOTAL PREVIOUS PAGE _____

Shipping — $5.00 for 1st book, $1.00 each additional _____

Illinois residents add 6.75% sales tax _____

Connecticut residents add 6.00% sales tax _____

TOTAL _____

To order, call Sourcebooks at 1-800-432-7444 or FAX (630) 961-2168 (Bookstores, libraries, wholesalers—please call for discount)

Prices are subject to change without notice.